DEVOUR NYC

A COOKBOOK

DEVOUR
NYC
A COOKBOOK

Discover the Most Delicious, Epic
and Occasionally Outrageous Foods of New York City

GREG REMMEY AND REBECCA WEST-REMMEY

Creators of @DEVOURPOWER

PAGE STREET
PUBLISHING CO.

PAGE STREET
PUBLISHING CO.

Copyright © 2021 Greg Remmey and Rebecca West-Remmey
First published in 2021 by
Page Street Publishing Co.
27 Congress Street, Suite 105
Salem, MA 01970
www.pagestreetpublishing.com

Distributed by Macmillan, sales in Canada by The Canadian Manda Group.

25 24 23 22 21   1 2 3 4 5

ISBN-13: 978-1-64567-197-8
ISBN-10: 1-64567-197-6

Library of Congress Control Number: 2019957343

Cover and book design by Molly Gillespie for Page Street Publishing Co.
Photography by Ken Goodman

Printed and bound in China

This book is dedicated to anyone who has looked at a photo of a **DEVOUR**-worthy dish and thought, "Damn, that's aggressive. I want that!" We're here for you.

CONTENTS

#DEVOURPOWER

Foreword by Adam Richman | 11
Introduction | 13

CHAPTER 1

AGGRESSIVE HANDHELDS | 15
OVER-THE-TOP SANDWICHES

Pepperoni Pizza Cheesesteak by The Truffleist | 16
The Butch Hero by Anthony & Son Panini Shoppe | 19
Loaded Doritos® Grilled Cheese by Harlem Public | 20
Philly Cheesesteak by Fedoroff's Roast Pork | 23
The Panino Supremo Sandwich by Blue Ribbon Fried Chicken | 24
Pulled Chicken Sandwich by Brine Chicken | 27
Smashed Plantain Patacon with Roast Pork by Cachapas y Mas | 29
Chopped Cheese Hero by Chef Papi Kitchens | 33
Sake-Battered Fish & Chips Sando by Silver Light Tavern | 34

CHAPTER 2

NOT YOUR AVERAGE BACKYARD BBQ | 37
BURGERS TO BRAG ABOUT AND HOT DIGGITY DOGS

Mac & Cheese Burger and Fries by The Bedford | 38
Shrimp Big Mac 'n' Cheese Burger by Flip 'N Toss | 41
Texas Hotdog by Dyckman Dogs | 44
Beer Cheese Burger by Benson's | 47
Wake and Bake Burger by Harlem Public | 48
Chili Cheeseburger by New York Burger Co. | 51
Scrapple & Egg Burger by Wing Jawn @ Echo Bravo | 52
Bacon Onion Jam "Magic" Smash Burger by Pig Beach | 55
The Steez Dog by At the Wallace | 56

CHAPTER 3

TOMAYTO, TOMAHTO | 59
FUHGEDDABOUDIT
(SAID IN YOUR BEST-WORST NEW YORK ACCENT)

Burrata Pizza by Macchina | 60

Dominican Pizza by Chef Papi Kitchens | 63

Nashville Hot Chicken Pizza by Emmy Squared | 65

Buffalo Chicken Pizza by East Village Pizza | 69

Shrimp Scampi Pizza by Macchina | 70

Pepperoni Pizza Mac & Cheese by Flip 'N Toss | 73

Lobster Burrata Pasta by Bella Gioia | 74

CHAPTER 4

KEEPIN' IT SAUCY | 77
WACKY WINGS

Firecracker Wings by International Wings Factory | 78

Grilled BBQ Buffalo Wings with Alabama White Sauce by Pig Beach | 81

Mango Habanero Bacon Wings by Morgan's Brooklyn Barbecue | 84

Smoky Manhattan Wings by Holy Ground NYC | 87

General Tso's Pig Wings by Wing Jawn | 88

Charred Pork Ribs by Glaze Teriyaki | 91

CHAPTER 5

TORTILLA TIME | 93
TACO VIBES AND BADASS BURRITOS

Steak Burrito with Kettle Queso by Conmigo | 94

Loaded Carne Asada Quesadillas by Dos Toros Taqueria | 97

Bulgogi Cheesesteak Tacos by SET L.E.S. | 100

Pancake Burrito by Mom's Kitchen & Bar | 103

Impossible™ Tacos by Diller | 104

Mac Wrap with Smoked Pastrami by Cash Only BBQ | 107

CHAPTER 6

FIRE STARTERS | 109
NOT SO SMALL APPS

Dynamite Mac & Cheese Balls by Burger, Inc. | 111
Kentucky Fried Cauliflower with Hot Honey by Silver Light Tavern | 112
Extra Cheesy Garlic Knots by East Village Pizza | 115
Kale Pesto–Stuffed Burrata by The Bedford | 116
Chicken Tinga Nachos by Roebling Sporting Club | 119
Fries with the Works by Blue Ribbon Fried Chicken | 122
Bronson Fries by Fedoroff's Roast Pork | 125
Slow-Cooked Bourbon-Glazed Bacon by Del Frisco's Double Eagle Steakhouse | 126
Fried Pickles by Diller | 129

CHAPTER 7

TREAT YO SELF | 131
ALL THINGS SWEET

PB&J Chicken 'N Waffles by 375° Chicken 'N Fries | 132
Funfetti Cookie Cakes by Schmackary's | 135
French Toast Fritters by Roebling Sporting Club | 138
Wookies by Echo Bravo | 141
Milk 'N Chips by 375° Chicken 'N Fries | 142

Thank-Yous | 145
About the Authors | 147
Index | 148

FOREWORD

Eating—the act of it, the joy taken from it, the feeling of anticipating something delicious you're going to chow down on, the feeling of blissful, sleepy satiety after you've finished that last scrumptious morsel—is one of the most universally loved, talked about and cherished activities we, as humans, engage in. It's a celebration of being alive, of the wonder of flavors—the way they combine, the way those magic proprioceptors in our lips, nose and tongue send messages of complexity, pleasure and tingly jabs of spicy pain to our brain, evoking memories past, miles traveled and the passion of creating and consuming the magic in the edible world around us.

Simply put, eating delicious food is just freaking awesome. AND YOU KNOW IT.

Clearly searching for and consuming mouthwatering culinary creations is something I'm rather familiar with—heck, I built my career around it! And Greg and Rebecca, without question or pause, exemplify that same gustatory adventurousness, and tear into life (and psychotic cotton candy burritos) with the zeal we wish we all could, and share their journeys, their jaw-dropping, drool-inducing, seemingly endless stream of death-row dinners and cheat-day meals, with the rest of us, so that we might explore fork-first for ourselves and follow in their fabulous, foodie footsteps.

Though I knew Team Remmey from their adventures as @DEVOURPOWER on social media, we first met at a food event we were cohosting at the New York City Wine & Food Festival. As the old expression goes, "Trust not a chef who does not lick their own fingers." Well, neither should you trust a food curator who does not glow when sharing their culinary finds, nor dive in with toothsome glee to the succulent Chopped Cheese sandwich they brought to the affair in the first place.

They have done what many wish they could do: jumped off the wheel, left the rat race, left their jobs and proceeded to—simply put—eat the tastiest, yummiest, dankest shit on planet Earth. And (not unlike yours truly) found a way to magically make a living out of it!

In this tome, the @DEVOURPOWER team is giving you the keys to the NYC comfort food culinary kingdom. Giving you the benefit of their insights collected over hundreds of hours of research, travel, copious note-taking and careful observation. And what's more, they're wresting the keys from the restaurants that held them and putting you in the driver's seat, giving you the one-two punch of being both food porn creator AND consumer. The knowledge goes into your head, the food goes onto your plate, the pics go on your timeline, the food goes into your mouth and you go into a state of bliss, gratitude and joy that you are alive, you are hungry and you have the tools, the talent, the guidebook and yes, the Power to Devour.

Enjoy the journey. Eat passionately. Chew carefully.

Adam Richman
Brooklyn, New York, August 2020

INTRODUCTION

Have you ever had a burger that was just absolutely loaded? How about one with macaroni and cheese on top? Or a pile of juicy roasted shrimp? Combine that all together and you get the Shrimp Big Mac 'n' Cheese Burger from Flip 'N Toss in the West Village (page 41). Now let's talk hot dogs: How about adding some nacho cheese? Maybe you lay on the chili as well. Top it all off with some crispy, crunchy onion straws and you've got yourself the Texas Hotdog from Dyckman Dogs (page 44). Hungry yet? Welcome to *Devour NYC!*

We are Greg Remmey and Rebecca West-Remmey of @DEVOURPOWER. We're a NYC-based couple who loves to eat aggressively and experience new cultures, cuisines and destinations. We started our journey back in 2012, soon after we began dating. Fast-forward to today and we are beyond thrilled to be able to share all of our over-the-top food experiences for a living.

We've spent the past seven and a half years of our lives striving to find the most outrageous, DEVOUR-worthy dishes in New York City. There's no limit to the creativity of the chefs here in NYC, and we've put them to the ultimate test: creating at-home versions of their craziest recipes, all of which are over-the-top showstoppers. From insane burgers that are sandwiched between macaroni-and-cheese buns to wings that are so spicy they'll knock your socks off, we've tried it all—and we're delivering it straight into your home kitchen. This isn't your average cookbook; these recipes will challenge your taste buds and impress your guests.

In our never-ending search for our "favorite dishes," we discovered that many classics were being uniquely flipped and re-created as over-the-top, one-of-a-kind inventions, and we needed to share them with the world. That's when @DEVOURPOWER truly set off on our mouthwatering quest. Not everyone who follows us and loves the crazy dishes that we DEVOUR can get to the restaurants we feature, however, because of where they live. We like to think this cookbook will bridge the gap and deliver our favorite foods right into your home.

To get to this point, we visited the kitchens of our favorite hot spots throughout the boroughs of New York City and asked the chefs to share the recipes for their best, most iconic dishes. We've gathered them together in this book to bring you more than 50 recipes for incredible, delicious food. We then broke those recipes down step by step to better help you re-create these dishes at home. Get ready to transform boring pancakes into loaded breakfast burritos and roll up mango-habanero wings in crispy bacon. In the pages that follow, there will be ladles and ladles of melty cheese and an unfathomable number of calories, but we promise that it all will be worth it!

We began this cookbook journey because we wanted to share the incredible food that we get to experience every day with all of our amazing, dedicated followers, regardless of their zip codes. We reached out to some of the most talented, passionate chefs in the Big Apple, and the delicious results are now in your hands.

CHAPTER 1

AGGRESSIVE HANDHELDS

OVER-THE-TOP SANDWICHES

Sandwiches are the most common food in all the world. There are so many variations, and what one person might consider a sandwich may be something totally different to someone else. We know that you know a sandwich basically is anything between two slices of bread. But don't think that we'll be wasting your time with plain old PB&J and humdrum ham and cheese. In this chapter, we've curated what we consider to be NYC's most outrageous, most drool-worthy, most over-the-top creations to ever grace a loaf of bread.

We traveled all over New York City to acquire these unique recipes. Beginning in Brooklyn, we made pilgrimages to the city's BEST Italian panini shop, the source of NYC's top Philly cheesesteak and the home of a very distinctive fish and chips concoction (see pages 23 and 34). We stopped in Midtown to examine another cheesesteak, but one with an unexpected twist (page 16). Then we trekked all the way up to Harlem to grab a crazy-crispy-crunchy-cheesy sammy (page 20). Heading even farther north to Inwood, we sampled a Venezuelan treat turned iconic neighborhood staple, the Chopped Cheese Hero (page 33). And finally, we stopped in Chelsea and the Lower East Side for two ridiculous chicken creations (pages 24 and 27).

What can you expect? Well, without spoiling the surprises of this chapter, we will tease a few special ingredients that you'll encounter while creating these curious masterpieces at home: plantains, Doritos, pepperoni, copious amounts of melted cheese and a whole lotta sauce!

From freakin' fried chicken to ooey-gooey grilled cheese, these DEVOUR-able handhelds will forever change the way you think about sandwiches.

PEPPERONI PIZZA CHEESESTEAK

The Truffleist, Pop-Up, NYC

Jimmy Kunz launched his boutique truffle business, The Truffleist, in 2013. He branched out with appearances at seasonal pop-ups, where he sold killer New York–style cheesesteaks that *Time Out* called one of the Five Best Things to Eat at the Winter Village at Bryant Park. This guy took cheesesteaks, an already mouthwatering dish, and made them better by introducing a multitude of cheeses and pepperoni to add a little more zing. Melted all together and tossed onto a buttery bun, this masterpiece is something you'll want to prepare time and time again. "It's the best of both worlds," says Kunz, referring to the pizza-cheesesteak mash-up. If you want to get extra fancy with some fresh shaved truffles, by all means make it rain.

MAKES 1 SANDWICH •

2 cups (480 ml) whole milk

3 tbsp (42 g) butter, divided

2 tbsp (16 g) all-purpose flour

Pinch of nutmeg

½ cup (56 g) shredded Swiss cheese

1 large yellow onion, sliced

1 small green or red bell pepper, seeded and diced

2 oz (57 g) sliced pepperoni

1 tsp vegetable oil

½ lb (226 g) inside top round or ribeye steak, very thinly sliced

½ tsp kosher salt

½ tsp black pepper

¼ cup (28 g) shredded mozzarella and provolone cheese blend

1 (6-inch [15-cm]) rustic roll or demi baguette, split

¼ cup (60 ml) marinara sauce, warm

1 handful mini mozzarella balls

2 tbsp (13 g) grated parmesan cheese

In a heavy saucepan over medium-low heat, add the milk.

In a second saucepan over low heat, add 2 tablespoons (28 g) of butter. When the butter begins to bubble, add the flour and cook, whisking constantly, until the mixture turns lightly golden brown, about 4 minutes. Slowly add the hot milk to the butter and flour mixture, whisking constantly, to produce a smooth cream sauce. Allow the sauce to come up to a gentle simmer and cook, whisking occasionally, until it thickens, about 10 minutes. Whisk in the nutmeg and the Swiss cheese. Cover and keep warm over very low heat.

Place a large skillet over medium heat. Add the remaining 1 tablespoon (14 g) of butter, followed by the onion. Cook, stirring occasionally, until the onion turns golden brown, about 10 minutes. Add the bell pepper and cook for another 2 minutes. Remove from the pan and set aside.

To the same now-empty pan over medium heat, add the pepperoni and cook, turning halfway through, until it's crispy, about 2 minutes per side. Transfer to a paper towel–lined plate to drain.

Place a heavy cast-iron pan over high heat and allow it to preheat. When it's hot, add the oil followed by the steak. Season the meat with the salt and pepper and cook, turning halfway through, until it's fully cooked, about 1 minute per side. Reduce the heat to low and break the meat up into small pieces with two spatulas. Add ¼ cup (40 g) of the onion and pepper mixture to the meat (reserving any extra for another use) and stir to warm it through and combine. Top with the shredded cheese blend.

Transfer the meat and cheese mixture to the roll and top with the warm cheese sauce, marinara sauce, mozzarella balls and pepperoni. Finish with parmesan cheese and serve.

THE BUTCH HERO

Anthony & Son Panini Shoppe, Williamsburg, Brooklyn

A few years back, we stumbled across Anthony & Son Panini Shoppe, a 25-year-old Italian deli in Brooklyn that carries everything from fresh mozzarella and homemade pasta to cured meats and imported Italian cookies. What we didn't know at the time was that Anthony—who always greets guests by asking, "Wanna espresso?"—and his son Sabino would soon become the makers of one of our favorite sandwiches. Here's a taste of our beloved hero, The Butch, an irresistible combination of deli meats, bacon, cheese and creamy ranch dressing.

MAKES 1 HERO •

Nonstick cooking spray

3 slices bacon

1 small yellow onion, diced

4 slices pastrami, diced

4 slices pepper turkey, diced

3 slices pepper jack cheese

1 Italian hero bun, split

Ranch dressing

½ avocado, pitted and sliced

Place a medium skillet over medium heat. Lightly spray the pan with nonstick cooking spray. Add the bacon and cook, turning once halfway through, until it's fully cooked and crispy, about 4 minutes per side. Transfer to a paper towel–lined plate to drain. When it's cool enough to handle, dice the bacon and set aside.

Drain and discard all but 1 teaspoon of fat from the skillet. Place the skillet over medium heat and add the onion. Cook, stirring occasionally, until the onion softens and turns light brown, about 3 minutes. Add the diced pastrami, turkey and bacon, and cook, stirring to warm and combine, for 1 minute. Top the meats with the pepper jack cheese and let it sit to melt.

Meanwhile, slather both sides of the hero bun with ranch dressing. Arrange the avocado slices on the bottom of the bun.

When the cheese has melted, add the filling to the bun and enjoy.

LOADED DORITOS® GRILLED CHEESE

Harlem Public, Harlem, New York

Since opening in 2012, Harlem Public has been a staple in the Hamilton Heights neighborhood of Manhattan. The menu has so many unique and DEVOUR-worthy dishes, but this Loaded Doritos® Grilled Cheese is definitely one of our favorites. Chef Chad Vigneulle says the recipe was inspired by the potato chip–topped sandwiches he loved as a kid. "A lot of people think it was just some stoner dish I came up with, but honestly, there was a lot more thought put into it than that," he says. A plain old grilled cheese just won't cut it after you've experienced this masterpiece.

MAKES 1 SANDWICH . . . .

1 ripe avocado, halved and pitted

2 tbsp (32 g) store-bought pico de gallo

Kosher salt

Black pepper

1 tbsp (14 g) brown sugar

Pinch of garlic powder

Pinch of onion powder

Pinch of crushed red pepper flakes

3 slices thick-cut bacon

2 thick slices high-quality sourdough bread

2 tbsp (28 g) unsalted butter, softened

2 slices New York aged cheddar cheese

2 slices pepper jack cheese

2 slices Swiss cheese

2 slices American cheese

10 Doritos Nacho Cheese Flavored Tortilla Chips

Preheat the oven to 350°F (175°C). Line a baking sheet with parchment paper.

Use a spoon to scoop the flesh from the skins of the avocado and place it in a medium bowl. Add the pico de gallo and mash with a fork to break up the avocado and combine the ingredients. Add salt and pepper to taste. Cover and refrigerate until needed.

In a small bowl, add the brown sugar, garlic powder, onion powder and red pepper flakes and stir to combine. Arrange the bacon on the baking sheet. Evenly coat the tops of the slices with all of the sugar and spice mixture, making sure to press it into the meat. Bake until crispy, about 25 minutes. Remove from the oven and set aside.

Place a frying pan large enough to accommodate both slices of bread over medium heat. Generously coat one side of each slice with butter and place them butter side down on the pan. Add 1 slice each of cheddar, pepper jack, Swiss and American cheese to each slice of bread. Add all of the bacon to 1 slice of bread. Cook until the bread turns golden brown on the bottom and the cheese melts, about 5 minutes.

Remove both slices of bread to a cutting board. Spread all of the guacamole onto the slice of bread without the bacon. Generously top both slices with Doritos chips and combine the slices to form a sandwich. Smash the sandwich a little to break up the chips, cut it in half and serve.

PHILLY CHEESESTEAK

Fedoroff's Roast Pork, Williamsburg, Brooklyn; Financial District, New York

South Philly natives Dave and Stella Fedoroff made a huge splash at Brooklyn's weekly foodie festival, Smorgasburg, with their authentic Philly cheesesteaks. "I think they made an impression on the customers because it's extremely hard to find an authentic cheesesteak in New York," says Dave. "We're the only owners who were actually born and raised in South Philly." This cheesy, mouthwatering bad boy is made with USDA Prime Black Angus, melty cheese and hot cherry peppers for that extra kick. For us, it was love at first bite.

MAKES 1 SANDWICH

1 tbsp (15 ml) vegetable oil

1 small yellow onion, diced

½ lb (226 g) top round beef, preferably USDA Prime, very thinly sliced

Cheese Whiz (or 5 slices yellow American cheese)

1 hoagie bun, split

½ cup (60 g) sliced hot cherry peppers (optional)

In a large skillet over medium heat, add the oil, onion and beef. Cook, stirring and breaking apart the meat with a spatula, until the onion is soft and the beef is well done, about 5 minutes. Carefully pour off any accumulated fat.

Arrange the onion and meat into a bun-size pile, then slide it to one side of the pan and top with the Cheese Whiz or sliced cheese. While the cheese melts, add the hoagie bun, cut side down, to the open space in the skillet to warm. When the cheese is fully melted, remove the hoagie bun and fill it with the beef, onion and cheese mixture. Top with the cherry peppers (if using), cut the sandwich in half and enjoy.

THE PANINO SUPREMO SANDWICH

Blue Ribbon Fried Chicken, East Village, New York

We (and many others) believe that Blue Ribbon makes some of the best fried chicken in the city, which makes this one of the best chicken parm sandwiches in the city. The chicken is perfectly seasoned with a bit of garlic and then fried to golden perfection. This dreamy, two-fisted sammy is layered with warm marinara and super-stretchy, super-stringy mozzarella. What else could you possibly want in life? Keep an eye out for another incredible recipe from Blue Ribbon on page 122!

MAKES 1 SANDWICH . . . .

SPICY SEASONING MIX

2 tsp (5 g) smoked paprika

1½ tsp (9 g) salt

½ tsp garlic powder

½ tsp onion powder

½ tsp dried ground parsley

½ tsp dried ground basil

¼ tsp cayenne pepper

MARINARA

¼ cup (60 ml) extra-virgin olive oil

7 cloves garlic, thinly sliced

1 (28-oz [794-g]) can crushed tomatoes

1 tsp kosher salt, plus more as needed

¼ tsp dried oregano

¼ tsp crushed red pepper flakes

CHICKEN

2 egg whites

1 cup (125 g) all-purpose flour

½ cup (60 g) matzo meal

½ tsp baking powder

1 (4-oz [113-g]) chicken cutlet, pounded flat

2 cups (480 ml) soybean or vegetable oil

1 challah or brioche burger bun, split and toasted

2 slices mozzarella cheese

To make the spicy seasoning mix, combine all of the ingredients in a small container and mix well. Set aside until needed.

To make the marinara, in a medium saucepan over medium heat, add the olive oil. When the oil is hot but not smoking, add the garlic and cook, stirring occasionally, until they're golden brown, 1 to 2 minutes. Add the crushed tomatoes and their juices. Rinse the tomato can out with 1 cup (240 ml) of water and add that to the saucepan. Add the salt, oregano and red pepper flakes. Bring the sauce to a simmer and cook, uncovered, stirring occasionally, for 25 minutes. Taste and adjust the seasoning, adding salt as needed. Reserve ½ cup (120 ml) of the marinara sauce for the sandwich, and store the rest in the refrigerator for another use.

To make the chicken, put the egg whites in a shallow bowl. In a second shallow bowl, add the flour, matzo meal and baking powder and stir to combine. Dunk the chicken cutlet into the egg whites, allowing the excess to drip off. Dredge the chicken in the flour mixture, making sure to evenly coat it on all sides. Set aside.

In a large, heavy skillet or cast-iron fryer over medium-high heat, add the soybean or vegetable oil and heat to 350°F (175°C). Carefully add the chicken cutlet to the hot oil and fry until golden brown, about 2 to 3 minutes per side, or until an instant-read thermometer registers at least 165°F (75°C). Transfer to a paper towel–lined plate to drain. Generously shake some spicy seasoning mix over the cutlet.

Meanwhile, gently warm the reserved ½ cup (120 ml) of marinara in the microwave or on the stove.

To build the sandwich, place the fried chicken on the bottom of the bun and top with the remaining ½ cup (120 ml) of warm marinara sauce followed by the 2 slices of mozzarella. Add the top bun, cut the sandwich in half and enjoy.

PULLED CHICKEN SANDWICH

Brine Chicken, Chelsea, New York

Brined chicken was a foreign concept to us until our friend Joe LoNigro opened this awesome concept restaurant in Chelsea. Brine Chicken earns rave reviews not just for its tender, flavorful chicken, but also the incredible sauce selection. "We wanted a sandwich that would highlight our pulled chicken," says LoNigro. "I think customers have always been blown away by how much flavor they get in each bite." The chef recommends starting with thick-sliced brioche bread, buttering it edge to edge and giving it a good toast to help seal in all the juices from the coleslaw and chicken. The homemade chili garlic sauce kicks this sammy up 100 notches.

MAKES 4 SANDWICHES

BLACK PEPPER AIOLI

1 cup (240 ml) mayonnaise

2 tbsp (17 g) minced garlic

1 tbsp (14 g) kosher salt

1½ tbsp (9 g) black pepper

BLACKENED CHILI HOT SAUCE

1 tbsp (2 g) dried chili de arbol

4½ tbsp (10 g) dried ancho chili

½ cup (68 g) peeled garlic cloves
(see Chef's Note, next page)

3½ tbsp (49 g) kosher salt

1 cup (240 ml) water

½ cup (120 ml) + 3 tbsp (45 ml)
vegetable oil

GARLIC CONFIT

1 lb (454 g) peeled garlic cloves
(see Chef's Note, next page)

1 cup (240 ml) vegetable oil

1 tsp kosher salt

2 tbsp (30 ml) honey

CHILI GARLIC SAUCE

1 batch Blackened Chili Hot Sauce

1 batch Garlic Confit

1⅓ cups (320 ml) white vinegar

2 tbsp (28 g) kosher salt

To make the black pepper aioli, place the mayonnaise, garlic, salt and pepper in a blender or food processor and process until smooth, making sure to scrape down the sides a few times. Cover and refrigerate until needed.

To make the blackened chili hot sauce, place the chili de arbol and ancho chili in a small skillet over medium heat and cook, turning often, until they begin to brown, about 2 minutes. Add the toasted chilies, garlic, salt and water to a blender or food processor. Process on high until smooth. While the machine is running, add the oil in a slow, steady stream. Cover and refrigerate until needed.

To make the garlic confit, place a small saucepan over medium-low heat. Add the garlic followed by the oil. Sprinkle in the salt, stir in the honey and cook, stirring every 5 minutes, for 30 minutes. The garlic should be very soft when pierced with a knife. Strain out the garlic, reserving the oil. In a blender or food processor, add the garlic and process until smooth. If the mixture is thicker than peanut butter, add some of the reserved oil to thin it out. Cover and refrigerate until needed.

To make the chili garlic sauce, place the blackened chili hot sauce, garlic confit, white vinegar and salt in a blender or food processor and process until smooth, making sure to scrape down the sides a few times. Cover and refrigerate until needed.

(continued)

GRILLED COLESLAW

1 large head cabbage (green or napa), sliced into 4 large rounds

2 cups (480 ml) mayonnaise

2½ tbsp (37 ml) apple cider vinegar

2½ tbsp (37 ml) white wine vinegar

1½ tsp (6 g) granulated sugar

1¼ tbsp (18 g) kosher salt

1¼ cups (138 g) shredded carrots

¼ cup (15 g) chopped fresh parsley

PULLED CHICKEN

1 lb (454 g) boneless, skinless chicken breasts or thighs

10 tbsp (150 ml) Chili Garlic Sauce

ASSEMBLY

2 tbsp (28 g) butter, softened

8 thick slices brioche bread

PULLED CHICKEN SANDWICH (CONT.)

To make the grilled coleslaw, preheat a gas or charcoal grill or a stovetop grill pan to high heat. Place the cabbage on the grill and cook for 3 minutes per side. Remove from the grill and refrigerate for 30 minutes to cool. When the cabbage is completely cool, core and thinly shred it, discarding the core. In a large mixing bowl, add the mayonnaise, apple cider vinegar, white wine vinegar, sugar and salt and whisk to combine. Add the shredded cabbage, carrots and parsley and toss to combine. Cover and refrigerate until needed.

To make the pulled chicken, place the chicken and chili garlic sauce in a medium pan over medium heat. Bring it to a simmer, then turn the heat down to low. Cook, stirring every 5 minutes or so, until an instant-read thermometer registers 165°F (75°C), about 20 minutes. When it's cool enough to handle, remove the chicken to a cutting board, shred it with two forks, return it to the pan with the sauce, cover and set aside.

To assemble the sandwiches, place a grill pan or a large skillet over low heat. Butter one side of each slice of bread, place it butter side down in the pan and grill for 30 seconds (cooking in batches as needed). Rotate the bread 90 degrees and grill for an additional 30 seconds. Flip the bread and grill for 30 seconds on the unbuttered side. Rotate the bread 90 degrees and grill for an additional 30 seconds. The bread should be golden brown on the buttered side when ready. Remove to a cutting board and repeat with the remaining bread slices until they are all grilled.

Place 4 slices of grilled bread butter side down on the cutting board. Evenly coat each slice with black pepper aioli. Top each slice with one-quarter of the pulled chicken, one-quarter of the grilled coleslaw and the other piece of grilled bread. Cut each sandwich in half diagonally and enjoy.

CHEF'S NOTE: Look for containers of pre-peeled garlic cloves at your local grocery store to make prep easier and faster.

SMASHED PLANTAIN PATACON WITH ROAST PORK

Cachapas y Mas, Ridgewood, Queens; Washington Heights, New York

Venezuelan food was completely new to us until about four years ago, when we stopped by the Cachapas y Mas food truck in Brooklyn. Now it's one of our favorite cuisines. The dish that converted us was the patacon, a traditional Venezuelan sandwich that swaps the bread for fried plantains. "The patacon is a ubiquitous late-night street food from the city of Maracaibo, Venezuela," explains chef-partner Jesus Villalobos. "The region is known for eating plantains during most meals, so it was only natural to make the plantain a vessel for meats, cheeses and sauces." Cachapas y Mas has since opened two brick-and-mortar locations that make it easier than ever to enjoy their food.

MAKES 4 SANDWICHES

1 (6-lb [2.7-kg]) boneless pork shoulder

½ cup (120 ml) Worcestershire sauce

½ cup (120 ml) white wine

½ cup (120 ml) naranja agria (bitter orange marinade), such as Goya®

1 head garlic, minced

2 tbsp (24 g) adobo seasoning

2 tbsp (11 g) dried oregano

2 cups (480 ml) mayonnaise

½ cup (30 g) chopped fresh parsley

½ cup (8 g) chopped fresh cilantro

4 cups (960 ml) vegetable oil

4 green plantains, peeled and halved lengthwise

4 thick slices queso de freír (frying cheese)

4 lettuce leaves

1 medium tomato, sliced

Ketchup

Trim the excess fat off the exterior of the pork shoulder, making sure to leave a thin layer. Make a crosshatch of four or five shallow cuts in the fat, but do not go all the way into the meat.

In a medium bowl, add the Worcestershire sauce, white wine, naranja agria, garlic, adobo and oregano and stir to combine. Pour this marinade over the pork, cover and refrigerate for 12 to 24 hours.

In a blender, add the mayonnaise, parsley and cilantro and process until smooth. Cover and refrigerate this green sauce until needed.

An hour before cooking, remove the pork from the refrigerator to allow it to come to room temperature.

Preheat the oven to 325°F (165°C).

Remove the pork from the marinade and place it in a large roasting pan. Discard the marinade. Cover the pan tightly with aluminum foil and cook for 4 hours. Raise the oven temperature to 450°F (235°C). Remove the foil and cook for an additional 30 minutes. Remove from the oven and allow to cool slightly. When the meat is cool enough to handle but still very warm, roughly chop or shred it. Cover to keep warm until needed.

In a tabletop fryer or a large, heavy pot over medium-high heat, add the oil and heat to 250°F (120°C). Carefully add the plantain halves and cook until they're lightly golden brown, about 7 minutes. Remove them to a paper towel–lined plate to briefly drain. Working one at a time, shape the warm plantain halves into loose balls with your hands and then flatten in a parchment paper–lined tortilla press into about a 6-inch (15-cm) disc. Alternatively, smash the plantains on a flat surface using a large, heavy pan.

(continued)

SMASHED PLANTAIN PATACON WITH ROAST PORK (CONT.)

Raise the oil temperature to 400°F (205°C). Carefully add the smashed plantains and fry until they're nicely golden brown, about 3 minutes. If they don't all fit in the pot at once, work in batches. When each batch is done, remove them to a paper towel–lined plate to drain.

To the same oil, add the queso de freír and cook, turning the pieces halfway, until they're crispy and golden brown, about 4 minutes. When done, transfer them to a paper towel–lined plate to drain.

To assemble the sandwiches, top a fried plantain with ¾ cup (168 g) of shredded pork, 1 slice of fried cheese, 1 lettuce leaf, tomato slices, ketchup and green sauce, and top with the second plantain.

CHOPPED CHEESE HERO

Chef Papi Kitchens, Inwood, New York

Stephen "Chef Papi" Rodriguez has been a longtime favorite chef of ours because he whips up incredible dishes like this Chopped Cheese Hero, which is a staple at corner bodegas all over town. "The Chopped Cheese is essentially a chopped-up cheeseburger on a fresh Italian roll or hero," Rodriguez explains. "My famous stretchy cheese sauce had to be a part of this." Fun fact: We cohosted a New York City Wine & Food Festival event with Adam Richman, and the line for this exact sandwich was insane!

MAKES 1 HERO . . . .

PAPI'S SAUCE

½ cup (52 g) peeled and sliced cucumber

1 tbsp (15 ml) water

1 cup (240 ml) mayonnaise

1 cup (240 ml) ketchup

CHEESE SAUCE

1 tbsp (15 ml) extra-virgin olive oil

1 small white onion, finely chopped

1 small celery rib, finely chopped

¼ red bell pepper, seeded and finely chopped

2 cloves garlic, finely chopped

1 tsp kosher salt

1 tsp pepper

1 (14-oz [400-g]) can cream of mushroom soup (see Chef's Note)

1½ cups (360 ml) heavy cream

1 cup (112 g) shredded mozzarella cheese

1 cup (113 g) shredded sharp cheddar cheese

ASSEMBLY

1 tbsp (15 ml) extra-virgin olive oil

½ lb (226 g) ground beef (preferably Black Angus)

1 tsp kosher salt

1 tsp black pepper

¼ cup (60 ml) Papi's Sauce

ASSEMBLY (CONT.)

1 large Italian hero bun, split and toasted

1–2 cups (70–144 g) shredded iceberg lettuce

4 slices tomato

2 cups (480 ml) Cheese Sauce

To make Papi's sauce, place the cucumber and water in a blender or food processor and process until smooth. In a medium bowl, add the mayonnaise, ketchup and cucumber purée and stir to combine. Cover and refrigerate until needed.

To make the cheese sauce, place a medium saucepan over medium heat. Add the oil, onion, celery, bell pepper, garlic, salt and pepper and cook, stirring occasionally, until the onion turns translucent, about 5 minutes. Add the mushroom soup and cream and bring to a simmer. Reduce the heat to low, add the mozzarella and cheddar cheeses, and stir to combine. Cover and keep warm until needed.

Place a large skillet over medium-high heat. Add the oil, ground beef, salt and pepper and cook, breaking the meat apart with a wooden spoon, until it's nicely browned, about 7 minutes.

Spread ¼ cup (60 ml) of Papi's sauce evenly on the top and bottom of the hero bun. Dress the bottom half of the bun with the lettuce and tomato, add the cooked beef and the cheese sauce, and cover with the top bun.

CHEF'S NOTE: Use ready-to-serve canned cream of mushroom soup in this recipe, not condensed soup.

SAKE-BATTERED FISH & CHIPS SANDO

Silver Light Tavern, Williamsburg, Brooklyn

We love fish and chips so much that we devoted a good portion of one of our food-filled London excursions to tracking down the very best. Little did we know that one of our all-time favorite takes could be found in our own backyard. This killer concoction, devised by Silver Light Tavern owner Mike Krawiec and Chef George Rallis, reinvents the classic pub fare in sandwich form. "Fish and chips is a classic bar dish, but it's also kinda messy, so we decided to turn it into a sandwich with everything in one nice little package," explains Krawiec. The other big twist is the sake batter, which really marries the dish to the bar environment. The yuzu tartar sauce adds a hint of vivid tartness.

MAKES 1 SANDWICH

YUZU TARTAR SAUCE

6 oz (170 g) dried kelp

1 cup (240 ml) sake

4 cups (960 ml) mayonnaise

¾ cup (180 ml) rice wine vinegar

1 cup (150 g) finely chopped cornichons

1 cup (240 ml) yuzu juice

Kosher salt

BATTER

2 eggs, beaten

2 cups (480 ml) sake (including 1 cup [240 ml] reserved from rehydrating the kelp)

2 cups (480 ml) ice-cold water

6 cups (960 g) rice flour

Kosher salt

SALT AND VINEGAR CHIPS

3 cups (720 ml) canola oil

1 large russet potato (Chef prefers Kennebec), cut into 6 wedges

1 tbsp (15 ml) apple cider vinegar

1 tsp kosher salt

ASSEMBLY

½ lb (226 g) cod fillets

Dash of togarashi

1 potato bun, split

First, rehydrate the kelp by adding it to a medium bowl with the sake. Let it sit for 5 minutes. Drain the kelp and reserve the sake to use in the batter.

To make the yuzu tartar sauce, finely chop the rehydrated kelp and add it to a large bowl with the mayonnaise, rice wine vinegar, cornichons and yuzu juice. Stir to combine and season with kosher salt. Cover and refrigerate until needed.

To make the batter, place the eggs, sake and water in a medium bowl and whisk to combine. Add the rice flour and stir to combine. Season with kosher salt.

To make the salt and vinegar chips, in a tabletop fryer or large, heavy pot over medium heat, add the oil and heat to 275°F (135°C). Carefully add the potato wedges to the hot oil and cook for 11 minutes. Remove to a paper towel–lined plate to drain and cool slightly. Using a plate, smash each potato wedge until it's almost flat. Set aside until needed.

Raise the oil temperature to 350°F (175°C). Dip the cod pieces in the batter to coat and carefully add them to the hot oil. Cook, flipping the fish halfway through, until it's golden brown, about 2 minutes per side. Remove to a paper towel–lined plate to drain, and season with togarashi.

Carefully add the flattened potatoes to the hot oil and fry until golden brown, about 3 minutes. Remove to a paper towel–lined plate to drain and season with the apple cider vinegar and salt.

To assemble the sandwich, layer the bottom of the bun with the yuzu tartar sauce, fried fish and potatoes, and cover with the top of the bun.

CHEF'S NOTES: Yuzu juice can usually be found at Asian markets. If you aren't able to get it, a suitable substitute can be made by blending equal parts fresh-squeezed lemon juice and orange juice.

Togarashi is a common Japanese condiment that's a mixture of seven dried spices. You can find it in some supermarkets, Asian markets and online.

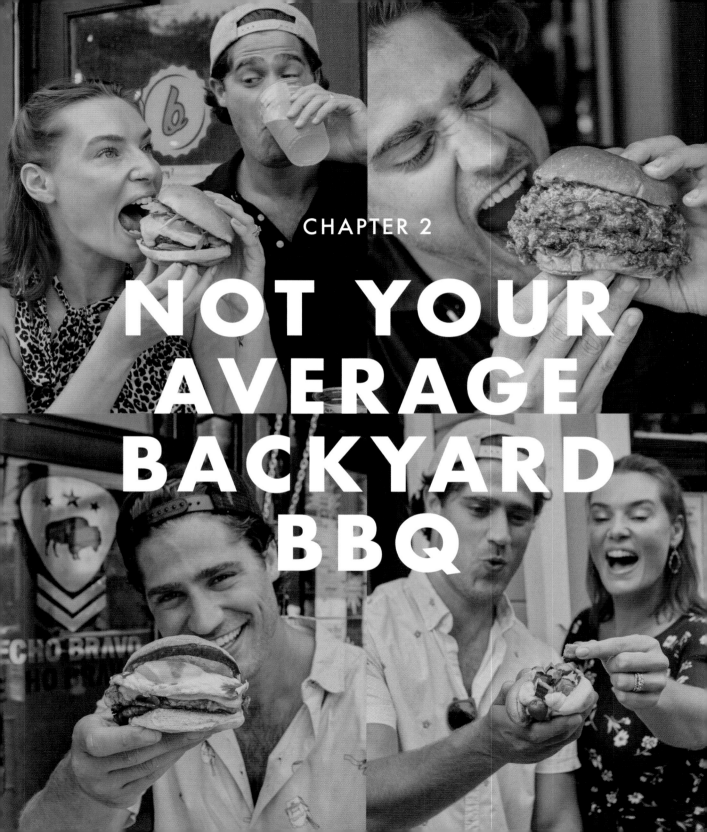

CHAPTER 2

NOT YOUR AVERAGE BACKYARD BBQ

BURGERS TO BRAG ABOUT AND HOT DIGGITY DOGS

If you follow us on social media, then you are likely aware that Greg's FAVORITE food is a damn good burger. To him, a damn good burger is super juicy, prepared medium-rare, dripping with sauce, loaded with toppings and, in some extraordinary circumstances, tucked into a macaroni-and-cheese bun. Rebecca agrees with him 100 percent, but needs the addition of blue cheese—something he will never understand!

In this chapter, you'll get a chance to swing up to Inwood to taste-test a famous Texas Hotdog loaded with nacho cheese, chili and crispy onions (page 44). While you're up there, stop in Harlem for the Wake and Bake Burger and fully loaded Steez Dog (pages 48 and 56). Take the West Side Highway down to Flip 'N Toss in the West Village for their incredible Shrimp Big Mac 'n' Cheese Burger (page 41). While you're on that side of Manhattan island, you can't skip the massive Chili Cheeseburger at New York Burger Co. (page 51). Then you can go across town to the East Village, where you can grab a bite of Benson's Beer Cheese Burger (page 47). You might be full to bursting, but don't stop yet! Next, we head out to Brooklyn for an over-the-top Mac & Cheese Burger, Scrapple & Egg Burger and Bacon Onion Jam "Magic" Smash Burger (pages 38, 52 and 55).

Now, let's get real. If you are anything like us, hot dogs and burgers were an everyday affair growing up. At countless backyard barbecues, we witnessed both weenies and patties being haphazardly tossed onto grills, where they were ignored and neglected until they were charred beyond recognition. When it came to condiments, all you got was ketchup, mustard, maybe a scoop of old relish. How boring is that? It's time to step up your grill game! For your next summer bash, impress your friends by cooking up one of these epic burgers or dogs. We've got your back.

MAC & CHEESE BURGER AND FRIES

The Bedford, Williamsburg, Brooklyn

Whenever friends and followers reach out to ask about our favorite New York City haunts, our response always includes The Bedford. When you visit, make sure to order this wild and wonderful sandwich that swaps humdrum hamburger buns for deep-fried macaroni-and-cheese patties. Once you bite into the crunchy, cheesy "buns," you'll understand why. The paprika aioli adds the perfect amount of spice without overwhelming your taste buds. "Everyone loves mac and cheese with their burgers, so we decided to combine them in the best way possible," says owner Sean Rawlinson.

MAKES 1 BURGER •

PAPRIKA AIOLI

1 tbsp (15 ml) mayonnaise

Juice of 1 lemon wedge

2 dashes sriracha sauce

½ tsp ketchup

½ tsp smoked paprika

½ tsp canola oil

Kosher salt

Black pepper

BLACKENING SEASONING

2 tbsp (14 g) smoked paprika

1 tbsp (5 g) cayenne pepper

1 tbsp (6 g) Tony Chachere's Original Creole Seasoning

1 tsp kosher salt

1 tsp garlic powder

1 tsp onion powder

1 tsp ground black pepper

½ tsp dried basil

½ tsp dried Greek oregano

FRIES

1 large russet potato

Kosher salt

Make the aioli first. In a medium bowl, add the mayonnaise, lemon juice, sriracha, ketchup and paprika and whisk to combine. Add the oil in a slow, steady stream while whisking to make an emulsion. Season to taste with salt and pepper. Set the aioli aside in the refrigerator until needed.

To make the blackening seasoning, combine all of the ingredients in a small container and mix well. Set aside until needed.

To make the fries, peel and rinse the potato. With a sharp knife and a steady hand, cut it into ¼-inch (6-mm)-thick sticks. Put the sticks in a medium bowl and add enough cold water to cover. Refrigerate until needed.

(continued)

MAC-AND-CHEESE BUNS

2 tbsp (36 g) salt

1 cup (115 g) uncooked elbow macaroni

¼ cup (28 g) shredded Swiss cheese

3 tbsp (19 g) grated parmesan cheese

¼ cup (28 g) shredded cheddar cheese

¼ cup (28 g) shredded mozzarella cheese

½ cup (120 ml) whole milk

2 tbsp (16 g) + ½ cup (63 g) all-purpose flour, divided

2 tbsp (28 g) butter, melted

½ tsp smoked paprika

½ tsp dried oregano

½ tsp garlic powder

½ tsp onion powder

2 eggs

½ cup (28 g) panko bread crumbs

½ tsp Blackening Seasoning

Kosher salt

Black pepper

4 cups (960 ml) canola oil

BURGER

1 tbsp (15 ml) canola oil

1 (6-oz [170-g]) beef patty

Kosher salt

Black pepper

1 slice cheddar cheese

MAC & CHEESE BURGER AND FRIES (CONT.)

To make the mac-and-cheese buns, add the salt to a large pot of water and bring to a boil over high heat. Add the macaroni and cook until al dente, about 1 minute less than the package directions. Drain, rinse with cold water, drain again and set aside.

In a medium bowl, add the Swiss, parmesan, cheddar and mozzarella cheeses and toss to combine. Place a large, heavy saucepan over medium-low heat and add the milk to warm. Slowly add the mixed cheeses by the handful to the milk, stirring constantly. When all the cheese has been added to the pan, slowly add 2 tablespoons (16 g) of flour, stirring constantly. Add the cooked macaroni and stir to coat. Add the butter, paprika, oregano, garlic powder and onion powder and stir to combine. Remove the pan from the heat.

Grease a sheet pan. Spread the macaroni mixture evenly on the pan in the approximate shape and size of two round bun halves. Cover with parchment paper and place in the freezer for 1 hour. When it's fully chilled, remove the pan from the freezer, remove the parchment paper and, using a large metal biscuit or cookie cutter, cut out two hamburger bun–size rounds. You could also use a knife to trim the sides into two even rounds.

Put the remaining ½ cup (63 g) of flour in a shallow bowl. Put the eggs in another shallow bowl and beat them lightly. Put the panko in a third shallow bowl, and add the blackening seasoning and a good pinch of salt and pepper. Working with one mac-and-cheese round at a time, dredge it in the flour, making sure to evenly coat it on all sides. Dip the round in the beaten eggs, allowing the excess to drip off. Finally, dredge it in the panko, making sure to evenly coat it. Repeat with the remaining bun half. Put both rounds on the sheet pan and refrigerate until needed.

In a tabletop fryer or a large, heavy pot over medium-high heat, heat the oil to 350°F (175°C). Carefully add the macaroni bun rounds and fry until they're golden brown, about 4 minutes. Fry one at a time if your pot isn't large enough to hold both at once. Transfer to a paper towel–lined plate to drain.

Drain and towel dry the potatoes and carefully add them to the hot oil. Cook until they're golden brown and crisp, about 7 minutes. Transfer to a paper towel–lined plate to drain and season with salt.

To make the burger, place a large, heavy skillet or griddle pan over medium-high heat. Drizzle the pan with the canola oil. Season both sides of the burger patty with salt and pepper and place in the pan. Cook until a nice crust forms on the bottom, about 3 minutes. Flip and cook the other side for 2 minutes. Top the burger with cheddar cheese, cover and cook until a nice crust forms on the bottom and the cheese is melted, about 1 additional minute for medium doneness.

To assemble, place the burger patty on one of the macaroni buns, spread 1 tablespoon (15 ml) of aioli on the top bun, and combine to form a sandwich. Serve immediately with the fries.

SHRIMP BIG MAC 'N' CHEESE BURGER
Flip 'N Toss, West Village, New York

Flip 'N Toss owner David Thual already had a hit on his hands with the Big Mac 'n' Cheese Burger, a massive, overflowing, over-the-top combination of macaroni and cheese and a double hamburger. But then he got the itch to create a surf-and-turf version, and this delicious monster was born. Four different cheeses are used for the mac-and-cheese part alone, which is crowned with juicy roasted shrimp. This recipe makes a lot of mac and cheese. When assembling the burger, don't be stingy with it—you want it to overflow onto the plate.

MAKES 1 BURGER •

SHRIMP SAUCE

1 tbsp (15 ml) extra-virgin olive oil

1 tbsp (15 ml) fresh lime juice

1 clove garlic, chopped

2 tbsp (8 g) chopped fresh parsley

2 tbsp (2 g) chopped fresh cilantro

Dash of smoked paprika

MACARONI AND CHEESE

2 cloves garlic, unpeeled

2 medium shallots, unpeeled

1 tbsp (15 ml) extra-virgin olive oil

2 tbsp (36 g) salt

3 cups (345 g) uncooked elbow macaroni

3 cups (720 ml) heavy cream

½ cup (57 g) shredded yellow cheddar cheese

¼ cup (28 g) shredded pepper jack cheese

1 tbsp (2 g) fresh thyme leaves

Kosher salt

Black pepper

¼ cup (28 g) shredded Monterey jack cheese

¼ cup (28 g) shredded white cheddar cheese

To make the shrimp sauce, place the olive oil, lime juice, garlic, parsley, cilantro and paprika in a small bowl and stir to combine. Cover and refrigerate until needed.

Preheat the oven to 350°F (175°C).

To make the macaroni and cheese, place the whole unpeeled garlic cloves and shallots on a small piece of aluminum foil, drizzle with the olive oil, wrap them up in the foil and roast in the oven for 30 minutes. Remove and let cool a bit, then peel them. Keep the oven on—you'll use it to bake the shrimp.

While the garlic and shallots are roasting, add the salt to a large pot of water and bring to a boil over high heat. Add the macaroni and cook until al dente, about 1 minute less than the package directions. Drain and set aside.

In a large saucepan over medium heat, add the cream and the yellow cheddar and pepper jack cheeses, stirring to combine. When the cheese has melted, add the thyme and the peeled roasted garlic and shallots, mashing them with a fork to incorporate into the sauce. Season to taste with kosher salt and pepper. Add the cooked macaroni and stir to combine. Add the Monterey jack and white cheddar cheeses and stir to combine. Cover and keep warm.

(continued)

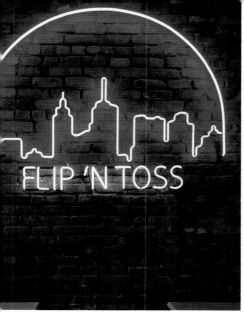

FLIP 'N TOSS

BURGER

5 large raw shrimp, peeled and deveined

2 (5-oz [142-g]) beef patties

Kosher salt

Black pepper

2 slices yellow American cheese

1 tomato slice

1 lettuce leaf

1 brioche bun, split and toasted

SHRIMP BIG MAC 'N' CHEESE BURGER (CONT.)

Place the shrimp on a sheet pan and toss with shrimp sauce. Roast the shrimp in the oven until they're cooked through, about 5 minutes.

To make the burger, preheat a gas or charcoal grill or a stovetop grill pan to medium-high, or place a large, heavy skillet or griddle over medium-high heat. Season both sides of the patties with salt and pepper and place on the griddle. Cook until a nice crust forms on the bottom, about 3 minutes. Flip and cook the other side until a nice crust forms, about 3 minutes for medium doneness. Top each patty with a slice of American cheese.

To assemble the burger, place the tomato, lettuce, one beef patty and a few spoonsful of macaroni and cheese on the bottom of the bun. Add the second beef patty and more macaroni and cheese. It should spill over the sides of the burger and onto the plate. Top with four of the roasted shrimp and the top bun. Add a toothpick with one shrimp on top of the burger to garnish, and enjoy.

TEXAS HOTDOG

Dyckman Dogs, Inwood, New York

This is New York, and in this town we can't get enough pizza, bagels and, obviously, hot dogs. Dyckman Dogs is a sister establishment to Cachapas y Mas, home of the Smashed Plantain Patacon with Roast Pork (page 29) dished up in chapter 1. What we really love about this Texas Hotdog is the hearty chili that sits between the dog and the bun, plus there's an extra crunch that comes from the French's® Crispy Fried Onions that top the warm melted nacho cheese. "The use of high-quality ingredients is the defining factor and makes our Texas dog stand out," says Chef Jesus Villalobo. "People appreciate a classic done right." While the chef prefers hotdogs from The Brooklyn Hot Dog Company, he says Hebrew National® makes a fine substitute.

MAKES 1 HOTDOG •

CHILI

¼ cup (60 ml) vegetable oil

1 medium yellow onion, chopped

1 red bell pepper, seeded and chopped

1 green bell pepper, seeded and chopped

4 cloves garlic, chopped

2 lbs (907 g) 80/20 ground beef

1 tbsp (14 g) kosher salt

2 tbsp (14 g) sweet paprika

2 tbsp (17 g) garlic powder

2 tbsp (14 g) onion powder

4 tbsp (32 g) chili powder

1 tbsp (8 g) ground cumin

1 tsp cayenne pepper

4 cups (960 ml) beef stock

2 tsp (10 g) tomato paste

1 (15-oz [425-g]) can tomato sauce

1 (28-oz [794-g]) can crushed tomatoes

1 (15-oz [425-g]) can pinto beans, drained

ASSEMBLY

1 large all-beef hotdog

½ cup (120 ml) water

Jarred nacho cheese sauce

ASSEMBLY (CONT.)

Butter

1 hotdog bun, preferably split-top brioche

French's Crispy Fried Onions

1 scallion, green part only, thinly sliced

To make the chili, in a large, heavy pot over medium heat, add the oil. When it's hot, add the onion, red and green peppers and garlic, and cook, stirring occasionally, until they're lightly browned, about 5 minutes. Remove the sautéed vegetables from the pot and set aside. To the same pot, add the ground beef and cook, breaking the meat apart with a wooden spoon, until it's nicely browned, about 7 minutes. Add the salt, paprika, garlic powder, onion powder, chili powder, cumin, cayenne and sautéed vegetables and cook for 1 minute while stirring. Add the beef stock, tomato paste, tomato sauce and crushed tomatoes. Bring to a simmer and cook, uncovered, stirring occasionally, for 25 minutes. Add the pinto beans and cook for 5 minutes.

To assemble the hotdog, in a medium skillet over high heat, add the hot dog and water and cook, uncovered, turning frequently, until the water has evaporated and the hotdog's exterior is dark and crispy, about 5 minutes.

While the hotdog is cooking, warm the nacho cheese sauce in a small saucepan over medium-low heat. Heat a separate skillet over medium heat. Butter the top and bottom (or the interior) of a split-top hotdog bun and place it butter side down in the skillet to toast. When the hotdog is done, place it in the toasted bun and top with some chili, warm nacho cheese sauce, fried onions and scallion.

CHEF'S NOTE: This chili recipe obviously makes more than you'll need for one hot dog. You can top the chili with some white onion and shredded cheese and eat it on its own. It should keep for about 5 days in the refrigerator or 1 month or so in the freezer.

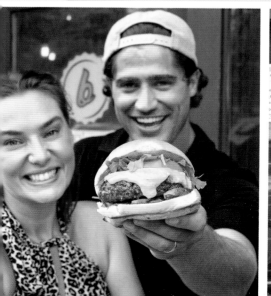

BEER CHEESE BURGER

Benson's, Lower East Side, New York

We can't put it any better than Aussie owners Annie Morton and David Peterson, who proclaim, "Everything is better with more cheese, more sauce and more avocado!" This zippy recipe caps a flavorful burger with spicy beer cheese, creamy avocado and fiery jalapeños. The best part? There will be plenty of beer left over from the recipe that you can sip while you whip, so to speak. By the way, the beer cheese recipe is amazing on its own as a dip for any and all occasions. This recipe makes enough for two burgers, but we recommend doubling, tripling or even quadrupling the quantities to produce a larger batch for your friends or family.

MAKES 2 BURGERS ●

BEER CHEESE

2 slices white onion

½ clove garlic

⅛ tsp cayenne pepper

2 tsp (10 g) butter

2 tsp (6 g) all-purpose flour

2 tbsp (30 ml) + 2 tsp (10 ml) lager beer

4 tsp (20 ml) heavy cream

½ cup (57 g) shredded cheddar cheese

Kosher salt

Black pepper

BURGERS

1 lb (454 g) beef short rib, freshly ground

⅛ tsp garlic powder

⅛ tsp onion powder

2 tsp (10 ml) stout beer

Kosher salt

Black pepper

2 rolls, split and toasted

Your favorite barbecue sauce

½ avocado, pitted and sliced

1 jalapeño pepper, seeded and diced

2 tomato slices

Handful of arugula

To make the beer cheese, place the onion, garlic and cayenne in the bowl of a blender or food processor and process until smooth.

In a medium saucepan over low heat, melt the butter. Add the puréed onion and garlic and cook until they begin to give off liquid and turn translucent, about 5 minutes. Add the flour and stir to combine. Add the beer, bring to a boil and add the heavy cream. Bring to a boil again, reduce the heat to low and slowly add the cheese. Stir continuously for 5 minutes. Season to taste with salt and pepper. Keep warm over a very low flame.

To make the burgers, place the ground beef, garlic powder, onion powder and beer in a medium mixing bowl and mix with your hands until they're evenly combined. Form the meat into two firm patties.

Preheat a gas or charcoal grill or a stovetop grill pan to medium-high. Season both sides of the burgers with salt and pepper and place on the grill. Cook until a nice crust forms on the bottom, about 3 minutes. Flip and cook the other side until a nice crust forms, about 3 minutes for medium doneness. While the burgers are cooking, toast both halves of the buns on the grill.

To assemble the burgers, smear some barbecue sauce on the bottom buns and top with avocado, jalapeño and the cooked patties. Smother the burgers with beer cheese sauce, then top with tomato, arugula and the top buns.

CHEF'S NOTE: Most butcher shops will grind beef short rib to order. If you don't have access to one who will, substitute 80/20 ground beef.

WAKE AND BAKE BURGER

Harlem Public, Harlem, New York

Chad Vigneulle, the chef and owner of Harlem Public, was inspired to come up with this meaty breakfast sandwich after an all-too-familiar situation. "I wanted to make a quality breakfast-style burger using all of my favorite breakfast items that I could eat when I woke up hungover as hell from closing the bar down the night before," he says. We've all been there, chef! This egg-topped breakfast burger is messy, greasy and jam-packed with big flavors, so it's guaranteed to slay that hangover!

MAKES 1 BURGER •

½ lb (226 g) ground beef (50 percent chuck, 50 percent brisket)

½ cup (114 g) unsalted butter, softened

2 tbsp (30 ml) maple syrup

3 tbsp (45 ml) mayonnaise

1 tbsp (15 ml) puréed chipotle peppers in adobo sauce

2 tbsp (28 g) brown sugar

½ tsp crushed red pepper flakes

½ tsp garlic powder

½ tsp onion powder

2 slices thick-cut bacon

1 frozen hash brown patty

1 brioche bun, split

2 tbsp (30 ml) canola oil

Kosher salt

Black pepper

1 slice New York State cheddar cheese

1 egg

Form the ground beef into a hamburger patty, making sure not to pack it too firmly. Refrigerate until needed.

In a small bowl, add the butter and maple syrup and whisk to combine. Set aside. In a separate small bowl, add the mayonnaise and puréed chipotle peppers in adobo sauce and whisk to combine. Set aside.

Preheat the oven to 350°F (175°C).

In another small bowl, add the brown sugar, red pepper flakes, garlic powder and onion powder and stir to combine. Arrange the bacon on a sheet pan and evenly coat the tops of the slices with all of the sugar and spice mixture, making sure to press it into the meat. Bake for 5 minutes. Place the hash brown patty on the same sheet pan as the bacon and continue baking for 15 more minutes, until the hash brown patty is golden brown and the bacon is crispy.

While the bacon and hash browns are baking, place a large skillet over medium heat. Liberally apply the maple butter to the top and bottom bun and place it, butter side down, in the pan. Toast until it's golden brown, about 2 minutes. Remove and set aside.

Increase the heat to high and add the canola oil. Liberally season both sides of the hamburger patty with salt and pepper and cook until a nice crust forms on the bottom, about 3 minutes. Flip and cook the other side until a nice crust forms, about 3 minutes for medium doneness. Top the patty with a slice of cheddar, cover the pan and allow the cheese to melt. Remove the burger and cover to keep warm.

Reduce the heat to medium and add the egg. Cook until the white is completely set but the yolk is still runny, about 2 minutes.

Liberally spread the chipotle mayo on the top and bottom buns. To the bottom bun add the hash brown, burger patty, bacon and fried egg. Top with the remaining bun and enjoy.

CHEF'S NOTE: Most butcher shops will grind chuck and brisket to order. If you don't have access to one who will, substitute 80/20 ground beef.

CHILI CHEESEBURGER

New York Burger Co., Chelsea, New York

Owner Christos Zisimatos knows what Americans crave, and that's a meaty hamburger topped with cheese and chili. "It's a whole lot of flavor topped with more flavor," he announces. The chili can be as spicy or tame as you prefer by taste-testing the hot peppers before tossing them in the pot. This cheeseburger is super-messy, so make sure you have plenty of napkins standing by! You also might need a nap after—just sayin'.

MAKES 1 BURGER •

BURGER SEASONING

1 tbsp (14 g) kosher salt

2 tsp (5 g) onion powder

1 tsp ground black pepper

CHILI

1 lb (454 g) 80/20 ground beef

⅓ cup (80 ml) vegetable oil

1 cup (160 g) chopped onion

1 clove garlic, minced

¼ cup (37 g) chopped red bell pepper

¼ cup (25 g) chopped poblano pepper

¼ cup (25 g) chopped jalapeño pepper (seeds and stems removed if you want less heat)

1 (14.5-oz [411-g]) can diced tomatoes, puréed

1 tbsp (8 g) ancho chili powder

1 tbsp (8 g) New Mexico chili powder

½ tbsp (4 g) ground cumin

½ tbsp (3 g) dried oregano

½ cup (120 ml) beef broth

2 tbsp (15 g) masa flour

1 (16-oz [454-g]) can kidney beans, drained

1 tbsp (1 g) chopped fresh cilantro

Kosher salt

Black pepper

CHEESEBURGER

1 (6-oz [170-g]) 80/20 beef patty

1 slice aged cheddar cheese

1 burger bun, split and toasted

To make the burger seasoning, place the salt, onion powder and pepper in a small container and stir to combine. Set aside until needed.

In a large pot over medium-high heat, add the ground beef and cook, breaking the meat apart with a wooden spoon, until it's nicely browned, about 7 minutes. Remove the meat and set aside. Drain and discard the beef fat.

To the same pot, add the oil, onion, garlic, bell, poblano and jalapeño peppers and cook, stirring occasionally, until the onion turns translucent, about 5 minutes. Add the tomatoes, ancho and New Mexico chili powders, cumin, oregano and browned beef. Reduce the heat to low and simmer uncovered, stirring occasionally, for 1 hour.

In a medium bowl, whisk the broth and masa flour to combine. Add this mixture and the kidney beans to the chili and cook for 15 minutes. Add the cilantro and season to taste with salt and pepper.

Preheat a gas or charcoal grill or a stovetop grill pan to medium-high heat. Season both sides of the beef patty with the burger seasoning and cook until a nice crust forms on the bottom, about 3 minutes. Flip and cook the other side until a nice crust forms, about 3 minutes for medium doneness. Top with the cheddar cheese, then place the patty on the bottom bun. Top with chili and the top bun and enjoy.

SCRAPPLE & EGG BURGER

Wing Jawn @ Echo Bravo, Bushwick, Brooklyn

This unique burger creation merges breakfast and dinner into one magical meal. Scrapple and eggs, traditional breakfast foods, get paired with a beef patty to great effect. The crispy fried onions give this dish a salty crunch, while the maple syrup adds the perfect kiss of sweetness. The only question that remains is: Will you cook your eggs runny or firm? We say, if you don't have a messy egg on a breakfast burger, did you really even brunch?

MAKES 4 BURGERS •

1½ lbs (680 g) 80/20 ground beef

1 tbsp (15 ml) Worcestershire sauce

1½ tsp (9 g) seasoned salt

1 tsp garlic powder

½ tsp ground black pepper

4 (½-inch [13-mm]-thick) slices scrapple

4 eggs

4 slices American (or your favorite) cheese

2 tbsp (28 g) unsalted butter

4 hamburger buns, split

2 tbsp (30 ml) maple syrup

1 (6-oz [170-g]) can crispy fried onions

Hot sauce (optional)

In a large mixing bowl, add the ground beef, Worcestershire sauce, seasoned salt, garlic powder and pepper. Using your hands, mix the ingredients until they are just combined. Portion the beef into four ¾-inch (2-cm)-thick burger patties.

Place a large griddle or two large skillets over medium-high heat. Place the scrapple on the griddle and cook for 3 minutes per side. Meanwhile, place the burgers on the griddle too (or cook the burgers after the scrapple if there isn't enough space for everything) and cook for 3 minutes. Crack the eggs onto the griddle (or cook the eggs after the burgers if there isn't enough space for everything). Flip the burgers and continue cooking until the burgers are medium-rare, about 3 minutes. Top each burger with a slice of cheese. When the egg whites are set and the yolks are still runny, remove the eggs to a plate.

Butter the top and bottom buns, place them butter side down on the griddle and cook until they're golden brown, about 1 minute. Drizzle a little maple syrup onto each top bun.

Place the burgers on the bottom buns, top with crispy fried onions, scrapple, fried egg, hot sauce (if using) and the top bun.

BACON ONION JAM "MAGIC" SMASH BURGER

Pig Beach, Gowanus, Brooklyn

When Pig Beach chef and owner Matt Abdoo said he created a burger inspired by Chef Josh Capon's work at Gotham Burger Social Club, we said bring it on! The Culinary Institute of America grad says the secret to the success of these burgers is really no secret at all: "People love the bacon onion jam!" We love the smashed beef patties, which double the meat while doubling the fun. The addictive burgers are topped with a savory sauce, crunchy pickles and the best bacon onion jam you will ever taste.

MAKES 4 BURGERS ● ● ● ● ● ● ● ● ● ● ● ● ● ● ● ●

BURGER SAUCE

2 tbsp (30 ml) ketchup

2 tbsp (30 ml) yellow mustard

2 tsp (7 g) finely chopped white onion

BACON ONION JAM

1 tsp vegetable oil

5 slices bacon, diced

1 tsp unsalted butter

1 medium Vidalia onion, sliced

2 tbsp (30 ml) balsamic vinegar

3 tbsp (42 g) light brown sugar

¼ tsp chopped fresh thyme

¼ tsp kosher salt

¼ tsp ground black pepper

BURGERS

1 lb (454 g) ground beef (brisket and short rib blend)

4 tsp (20 ml) vegetable oil

Kosher salt

Black pepper

½ cup (120 ml) Bacon Onion Jam

8 slices yellow American cheese

¼ cup (60 ml) Burger Sauce

4 potato rolls (preferably Martin's®), split

24 bread and butter pickle chips

To make the burger sauce, place the ketchup, mustard and onion in a bowl and stir to combine. Set aside until needed.

To make the bacon onion jam, place a large skillet over medium heat and add the oil and bacon. Cook, stirring occasionally, until the bacon is crispy, about 8 minutes. Transfer to a paper towel–lined plate to drain. Discard (or reserve for another use) all but 2 tablespoons (30 ml) of the bacon fat in the skillet. Reduce the heat to medium-low, add the butter and onion, and cook, stirring occasionally, until the onion is lightly caramelized, about 15 minutes. Add the cooked bacon, vinegar, brown sugar, thyme, salt and pepper, and continue cooking until it reaches a jam-like consistency, about 10 minutes. Cover and refrigerate until needed.

Divide the ground beef into eight 2-ounce (57-g) balls and set aside.

Place a griddle pan or a large skillet over medium-high heat. When the pan is hot, add the oil. Place the beef balls on the griddle and, using a heavy metal spatula, smash them down to slider size. Season each burger with salt and pepper and top with 1 tablespoon (15 ml) of bacon onion jam. Cook, without moving, until the bottoms are well-browned and crisp, about 1 minute. Flip the burgers and top each with 1 slice of cheese. Continue cooking until the cheese is melted around the edges and the bottoms of the burgers are brown and crispy, about 2 minutes.

Meanwhile, spread ½ tablespoon (8 ml) of burger sauce onto each bottom bun. When the burgers are done, place two patties onto each bottom bun. Spread another ½ tablespoon (8 ml) of burger sauce onto the top buns, top each patty with 6 pickle slices, close the burgers and serve.

CHEF'S NOTE: Most butcher shops will grind brisket and beef short rib to order. If you don't have access to one who will, substitute 80/20 ground beef.

THE STEEZ DOG

At the Wallace, Harlem, New York

"Steez," according to co-owner Lauren Brie Lynch, is shorthand for "style with ease," as coined by rapper Method Man. The Steez Dog, as dished up by the great Harlem venue At the Wallace, is a breezy, cheesy mash-up that combines hot dogs and mac and cheese, all topped with a shower of crispy bacon bits. This beast is a bit messy, but so, so worth it. While elbow macaroni is the traditional pasta choice for mac and cheese, this kitchen prefers shells because they grab and hold the sauce so much better. Don't forget the ice-cold beer chaser.

MAKES 1 HOTDOG •

2 tbsp (28 g) kosher salt, plus more to season

½ lb (226 g) uncooked medium pasta shells

2 tbsp (28 g) butter

1 clove garlic, chopped

2 tbsp (16 g) all-purpose flour

1¼ cups (300 ml) whole milk

Black pepper

¼ cup (28 g) shredded cheddar cheese

¼ cup (28 g) shredded Monterey jack cheese

¼ cup (28 g) shredded Swiss cheese

¼ lb (113 g) slab bacon, chopped into ½-inch (13-mm) pieces

1 hot dog (preferably with natural casing)

1 potato hot dog bun, toasted

1 tsp sliced scallion

Add the salt to a large pot of water and bring to a boil over high heat. Add the pasta shells and cook until al dente, about 1 minute less than the package directions. Drain, rinse with cold water, drain again and set aside.

In a medium saucepan over medium-low heat, add the butter and garlic and cook until it's lightly browned, about 2 minutes. Add the flour and cook, stirring constantly, for 2 minutes. Add the milk in a slow stream while whisking constantly. Add a few pinches of salt and pepper. Reduce the heat to low and cook, stirring constantly, for 2 minutes, until thickened. Remove from the heat, add the cheddar, Monterey jack and Swiss cheeses, and stir to melt and blend. Add the cooked pasta and stir to coat. Cover and keep warm.

In a large skillet over medium-high heat, add the bacon and cook, stirring occasionally, until it's golden brown and crisp, about 8 minutes. Transfer to a paper towel–lined plate to drain. Discard (or reserve for another use) all but 1 tablespoon (15 ml) of the bacon fat in the skillet. Place the hot dog in the skillet and cook until the exterior is dark and crispy, about 5 minutes.

To assemble, place the hot dog in the toasted bun, top with macaroni and cheese, bacon and scallions.

CHAPTER 3

TOMAYTO, TOMAHTO

FUHGEDDABOUDIT (SAID IN YOUR BEST-WORST NEW YORK ACCENT)

Coming from Italian-American families, both of us adore pasta, sauce and meatballs more than most things. But after living for more than a decade in New York City, we have cultivated an unconditional fondness for pizza in all its many shapes, styles and configurations. What we appreciate about this specific culinary genre is the level of expertise it takes to master. Anyone can get the hang of making a platter of spaghetti and meatballs, but can you step up to these meticulously crafted pizza pies?

We stop in Gramercy for a pair of the most decadent pizzas we've ever tasted (pages 60 and 70). We then cruise way uptown to Inwood to try an awesome Dominican version of an Italian staple (page 63). From there we travel to the East Village to feast on a cheesy chicken pie with a kick (page 69). Heading over to the West Village, we casually whip up a pepperoni mac-and-cheese combo that will knock your socks off (page 73). Then we journey to Park Slope in Brooklyn, where luxurious lobster elevates a pasta dish above all others (page 74).

Why isn't Little Italy covered in this chapter, you might ask. Well, after years of searching for the best of the best, we're 100 percent convinced that the best Italian joints are the mom-and-pop shops sprinkled throughout all five boroughs of the city, including but not limited to touristy Mulberry Street. We think you'll agree.

BURRATA PIZZA

Macchina, Gramercy, New York

The only thing better than slicing into a ball of burrata is slicing into a ball of burrata sitting atop a freshly baked pizza. This pizza, courtesy of Chef Sean Rawlinson (who teaches us how to make burrata on page 116), features four types of cheese. The star of the show, however, is the burrata, which oozes its creamy core when sliced. We invite you to dip your pizza crust into the gooey goodness, like we do.

MAKES 1 PIZZA ●

TOMATO SAUCE

1 (28-oz [794-g]) can whole peeled tomatoes

1 clove garlic, grated

⅓ cup (80 ml) extra-virgin olive oil

1 tsp dried oregano

5 fresh basil leaves, chopped

1 tsp crushed red pepper flakes

1 tsp kosher salt

PIZZA

1 lb (454 g) prepared pizza dough

¼ cup (60 ml) Tomato Sauce

3 tbsp (21 g) shredded fresh mozzarella

2 oz (57 g) fior di latte, small-dice (see Chef's Notes)

2 tbsp (12 g) grated pecorino cheese

1 burrata ball (page 116, see Chef's Notes)

2 tbsp (5 g) thinly sliced fresh basil

Red and black Hawaiian salt

1 tsp extra-virgin olive oil

To make the tomato sauce, place all of the ingredients in a blender or food processor and process until smooth, making sure to scrape down the sides a few times. Set aside until needed.

Remove the pizza dough from the refrigerator. If you have a pizza stone, place it in the oven prior to preheating. You can also use a preheated baker's pan. Or a neat trick is to use a preheated cast-iron skillet, turn it over and the 10-inch (25-cm) round bottom is a perfect replacement for a pizza stone. Preheat the oven to 500°F (260°C).

Flour a pizza peel or a clean work surface and stretch the dough out to approximately 10 inches (25 cm). Working from the outside in, cover the pizza with tomato sauce. Evenly arrange the shredded mozzarella across the top. Scatter the fior di latte evenly around the pizza. Sprinkle the pecorino across the top and place the burrata in the center. Use the peel to transfer the pizza to the stone or pan in the oven. Or carefully remove the pan and use a metal spatula, or better yet a wide fish spatula, to move the pizza to the pan and return it to the oven.

Bake the pizza until the cheese has melted and the edges are golden brown, about 10 minutes. Sprinkle with the basil and the red and black Hawaiian salt, drizzle with the olive oil, slice and serve.

CHEF'S NOTES: Fior di latte is a type of mozzarella that can be found at higher-end grocery stores. If you aren't able to get it, you can substitute half fresh mozzarella and half ricotta, but they need to be made from cow's milk.

Using Sean's recipe for homemade burrata on page 116 will make for the most authentic—and delicious—experience with this pizza, but store-bought burrata will work well as a substitute. You can follow the plain burrata recipe without the pesto filling, but certainly if you are feeling fancy go all out by including the pesto filling!

DOMINICAN PIZZA
Chef Papi Kitchens, Inwood, New York

We love how creative Stephen "Chef Papi" Rodriguez is when it comes to combining classic New York City dishes with his Dominican roots. A perfect example is this Dominican-style pizza, which he serves up from his perch at Chef Papi Kitchens. "I wanted to honor that unforgettable New York pizza with a taste of my Dominican culture," Rodriguez explains. "Making the crust out of fried plantains was an exciting challenge, but it's definitely what makes this dish so unique." His biggest tip is to form the pizza crust while the mashed plantains are still warm. Use leftover chimichurri on grilled meats, roasted veggies and scrambled eggs, or as a spread for sandwiches.

MAKES 1 PIZZA ●

PAPI'S SAUCE
½ cup (52 g) peeled and sliced cucumber

1 tbsp (15 ml) water

1 cup (240 ml) mayonnaise

1 cup (240 ml) ketchup

CHIMICHURRI SAUCE
¼ small red onion, finely chopped

¼ red bell pepper, seeded and finely chopped

½ cup (68 g) fresh garlic cloves, finely chopped

½ bunch (28 g) Italian parsley, finely chopped

2 cups (480 ml) extra-virgin olive oil

¼ cup (60 ml) white vinegar

1 tbsp (14 g) kosher salt

TOMATO SAUCE
2 tbsp (30 ml) extra-virgin olive oil

7 cloves garlic, thinly sliced

¼ tbsp crushed red pepper flakes

1 tsp dried oregano

1 medium white onion, chopped

1 lb (454 g) pancetta, chopped

1 tsp kosher salt

1 tsp sugar

1 (28-oz [794-g]) can whole peeled tomatoes

1 cup (240 ml) heavy cream

To make Papi's sauce, place the cucumber and water in a blender or food processor and process until smooth. In a medium bowl, add the mayonnaise, ketchup and cucumber purée and stir to combine. Cover and refrigerate until needed.

To make the chimichurri sauce, place the onion, bell pepper, garlic, parsley, olive oil, white vinegar and salt in a large bowl and stir to combine. Cover and set aside at room temperature until needed.

To make the tomato sauce, place a medium saucepan over medium-high heat and add the oil. When the oil is hot, add the garlic, red pepper flakes, oregano, onion, pancetta, salt and sugar. Cook, stirring occasionally, until the onion turns translucent and the pancetta is golden brown, about 6 minutes. Add the tomatoes with their juice and bring to a simmer, crushing the tomatoes with a wooden spoon. Cook, stirring occasionally, for 30 minutes. Add the cream and continue cooking for 10 minutes. Remove from the heat, allow to cool and refrigerate until needed.

(continued)

PIZZA

½ cup (69 g) diced longaniza (Dominican sausage)

6 cups (1.4 L) canola oil, plus more for pan-frying

2 green plantains, peeled and cut into ¼-inch (6-mm)-thick slices

2 tbsp (30 ml) Chimichurri Sauce, divided

Kosher salt

1 boneless, skinless chicken breast, pounded thin

½ cup (120 ml) Tomato Sauce

1½ cups (168 g) shredded mozzarella cheese, divided

2 slices Dominican salami, halved

1 thick slice queso de freír (frying cheese), cut into 4 squares

½ cup (120 ml) Papi's Sauce

1 tbsp (4 g) chopped fresh Italian parsley

DOMINICAN PIZZA (CONT.)

To make the pizza, in a small skillet over medium heat, add the longaniza and cook, stirring occasionally, until crisp, about 6 minutes. Drain and refrigerate until needed.

In a large, heavy pot (large enough in diameter to accommodate the pizza crust) over medium-high heat, add the oil and heat to 350°F (175°C). Carefully add the plantain slices and cook until lightly golden brown, about 5 minutes. Remove them to a paper towel–lined plate to briefly drain. Maintain the oil temperature to fry the crust in the next step.

In a large bowl, add the fried plantains, 1 tablespoon (15 ml) of chimichurri sauce and a pinch of salt. Using a fork or a potato masher, mash until there are no large chunks remaining. Form the mashed plantains into a ball. Using your hands, flatten the ball into a large, thin 10- to 12-inch (25- to 30-cm) pizza crust. Carefully return the crust to the hot oil to crisp up, about 3 minutes. Remove to a cooling rack.

Preheat a gas or charcoal grill or a stovetop grill pan to medium-high heat. Coat the chicken breast in 1 tablespoon (15 ml) of chimichurri, season with salt and grill until the meat reaches an internal temperature of 165°F (75°C), about 3 minutes per side. Remove from the heat and cut into small cubes.

In a small saucepan over low heat, add the tomato sauce and the diced cooked chicken. Cover and keep warm until needed.

Preheat the oven to 500°F (260°C).

Evenly sprinkle ½ cup (56 g) of mozzarella cheese on the fried plantain pizza crust. Ladle on the warm tomato sauce with chicken. Sprinkle on the remaining 1 cup (112 g) of mozzarella cheese. Top with the fried longaniza and bake until the cheese is completely melted and the longaniza is sizzling, about 6 minutes.

Meanwhile, place a large skillet over medium-high heat. Add 1 tablespoon (15 ml) of canola oil followed by the Dominican salami and queso de freír and cook until both are crisp and golden brown, about 2 minutes per side. Remove to a plate.

Remove the pizza from the oven, cut into four slices and top each slice with 1 piece of salami and one piece of fried cheese. Drizzle with Papi's sauce and garnish with parsley.

CHEF'S NOTES: If you can't find longaniza, you can substitute linguica or chorizo.

You'll end up with more tomato sauce than you need for this pizza. Store the rest in the refrigerator and have pasta the next day.

NASHVILLE HOT CHICKEN PIZZA

Emmy Squared, East Village and Upper East Side, New York; Williamsburg, Brooklyn

After spending time in Nashville, Chef Matthew Hyland was inspired to create this mind-blowing deep-dish pizza starring—you guessed it!—Nashville hot chicken. "Spicy fried chicken has a universal appeal," says Hyland. "Putting it on a pizza is a fun way to serve it, and people love the creativity on a classic dish. The white sauce is vital in helping to tame the heat from the high-test chicken. And the pickles? Well, they don't need any explanation! For epic results, brine the chicken for at least 48 hours and ferment the dough for at least 24 hours. But, Hyland says, there is no shame in swapping out the homemade fried chicken for store-bought. His favorite? Popeyes®.

MAKES 1 PIZZA ●

BRINED CHICKEN

¾ cup (180 ml) buttermilk

2 tsp (3 g) cayenne powder

1 tsp kosher salt

1 tsp sugar

1 boneless chicken thigh, cut in half lengthwise into 2 long strips

DETROIT PIZZA DOUGH
(enough for 1 pizza)

¾ cup (180 ml) warm water (approximately 110°F [45°C])

1 tsp sugar

1 tsp active dry yeast

1½ cups (206 g) + 1 tbsp (9 g) unbleached bread flour (preferably King Arthur)

1 tbsp (15 ml) vegetable oil, plus more to grease the bowl

1 tsp kosher salt

NASHVILLE HOT SPICE
(about ½ cup [120 ml])

2 tsp (10 g) kosher salt

2 tsp (3 g) cayenne powder

1 tsp onion powder

1 tsp garlic powder

1 tsp ground cumin

1 tsp sweet, smoked or spicy Spanish paprika

NASHVILLE HOT SPICE (CONT.)

1 tsp sugar

1 tsp finely ground black pepper

⅓ cup (80 ml) vegetable oil

To brine the chicken, place the buttermilk, cayenne, salt and sugar in a medium bowl and stir to combine. Add the chicken, toss, cover and place in the refrigerator to brine for at least 48 hours.

To make the pizza dough, place the warm water, sugar and yeast in the bowl of a stand mixer and stir to combine. Let it stand until frothy, about 5 minutes. Add the flour. With the dough hook attachment in place, mix on medium speed until the dough forms a loose ball, about 30 seconds. Leaving the dough hook in place, cover the bowl with a kitchen towel for 10 minutes to allow the flour to fully hydrate.

Remove the kitchen towel and mix on medium-low speed until the dough is smooth, about 8 minutes, occasionally scraping down the sides of the bowl as well as the dough hook. The dough should be soft and sticky, but still pull away from the sides of the bowl. Increase the speed to medium-high and drizzle in the oil, mixing until it is incorporated, about 2 minutes. Add the salt and mix until it is well distributed, about 2 minutes. Lightly oil a bowl large enough to accommodate the dough as it expands. Transfer the dough to the oiled bowl, cover tightly with plastic wrap and place in the refrigerator to ferment for 24 to 48 hours.

To make the Nashville hot spice, place all of the ingredients in a medium bowl and stir well to combine. Cover and set aside until needed.

(continued)

WHITE SAUCE
(about ¾ cup [180 ml])

3 tbsp (45 ml) apple cider vinegar

1½ tbsp (23 g) sugar

¾ tsp kosher salt

¾ tsp ground black pepper

¾ tsp grated fresh horseradish

½ cup (120 ml) mayonnaise

FRIED CHICKEN PIZZA

1¾ cups (219 g) all-purpose flour

1 tsp kosher salt

1 tsp black pepper

¾ cup (180 ml) buttermilk

4 cups (960 ml) vegetable oil

½ cup (57 g) shredded mild cheddar cheese

½ cup (56 g) shredded mozzarella cheese

¾ cup (107 g) chopped dill pickles

NASHVILLE HOT CHICKEN PIZZA (CONT.)

To make the white sauce, place the apple cider vinegar, sugar, salt, pepper and horseradish in a medium bowl and stir to combine. Add the mayonnaise and stir to combine. Refrigerate until needed.

To make the fried chicken pizza, place the flour, salt and pepper in a shallow bowl and stir to combine. In a second shallow bowl, add the buttermilk. Remove the chicken from the brine, allowing the excess to drip off. Discard the brine. Dredge the chicken pieces in the seasoned flour, shaking off the excess. Dunk the chicken in the buttermilk, allowing the excess to drip off. Dredge the chicken pieces one final time in the seasoned flour.

In a tabletop fryer or a large, heavy pot over medium-high heat, add the oil. Heat to 350°F (175°C). Carefully add the breaded chicken to the hot oil and fry until golden brown, about 12 minutes, or until an instant-read thermometer registers 165°F (75°C). Remove the chicken with a slotted spoon and place directly into the Nashville hot spice mixture to coat. Cut each of the chicken pieces into 3, making 6 total pieces. Set aside until the pizza is done.

Preheat the oven to 525°F (275°C).

Remove the pizza dough from the refrigerator. Grease a 10 x 14–inch (25 x 35–cm) nonstick rectangular pan (or a well-seasoned black metal Detroit pizza pan if you happen to have one). Place the dough in the pan, then press and spread it so that it covers the bottom of the pan. If the dough springs back away from the edges, cover the pan with plastic wrap and wait a few minutes before trying again.

In a small bowl, toss to combine the cheddar and mozzarella cheeses. Sprinkle the cheese mixture on the pizza, making sure to apply most of it on and around the edges of the dough so that it comes into contact with the sides of the pan. This is what forms the "frico" crust that gives Detroit-style pizza its characteristic crispy, cheesy exterior. Scatter the remainder of the cheese evenly across the top.

Bake the pizza until the top is golden brown and the edges are crisp, about 10 minutes. Remove from the oven and let stand for 1 minute. Using a small sharp knife, loosen the pizza around all four sides. Using a wide metal spatula, transfer the pizza to a cutting board. Cut into 6 equal slices, top each slice with a piece of fried chicken, drizzle with white sauce and garnish with the chopped pickles.

BUFFALO CHICKEN PIZZA

East Village Pizza, East Village, New York

East Village Pizza is a staple in that neighborhood. Owner Frank Kabatas has a knack for creating dishes that go completely viral on social media, such as the Double-Stacked Pizza and Extra Cheesy Garlic Knots (see page 115). For this recipe, swing by your favorite Italian grocer or prepared foods store and pick up some refrigerated (or frozen) pizza dough and breaded chicken cutlets. If you want to make your own Buffalo wing sauce, just mix equal parts melted butter and hot sauce. Or you can grab a bottle off the shelf. The 2½ pounds (1.1 kg) of mozzarella is not a typo! This beast is loaded with melted cheesy goodness.

MAKES 1 PIZZA

1 lb (454 g) prepared pizza dough

3 pieces prepared breaded chicken cutlets

2 cups (480 ml) Buffalo wing sauce

2½ lbs (1.1 kg) shredded mozzarella cheese

Remove the pizza dough from the refrigerator and let it come to room temperature.

Preheat the oven to 500°F (260°C).

Cut the breaded chicken cutlets into ½-inch (13-mm) cubes, place them in a medium bowl and toss with the Buffalo wing sauce.

Spread the pizza dough onto a large round pizza pan. Sprinkle the cheese evenly across the top of the pizza. Evenly spread the chicken cutlet pieces on the pizza. Bake until the crust is golden brown and the cheese is melted and bubbling, about 15 minutes. Remove from the oven, slice into 8 pieces and enjoy.

SHRIMP SCAMPI PIZZA

Macchina, Gramercy, New York

Chef Sean Rawlinson knows how to get people's attention. On its own, the shrimp scampi in this recipe is garlicky, rich and delicious—but by placing it on top of pizza you reach an entirely different level. "We wanted to make an over-the-top pizza that combines two Italian staples," Rawlinson says. This dreamy dish is like the pizza version of dipping warm Italian bread into a creamy seafood sauce. It might be messier than a typical pizza, but it's absolutely worth the extra napkins. Chef warns against fully cooking the shrimp in the skillet or else they will wind up overcooked on the pizza.

MAKES 1 PIZZA •

1 lb (454 g) prepared pizza dough

2 tbsp (30 ml) extra-virgin olive oil

¼ cup (40 g) sliced shallots

½ tsp lemon juice

1 clove garlic, minced

¼ cup (60 ml) white wine

6 large shrimp, tails on, shelled and deveined

1 tsp lemon zest

Pinch of kosher salt

Pinch of black pepper

1½ oz (42 g) fresh mozzarella cheese, cubed

¼ cup (28 g) shredded mozzarella cheese

1 tbsp (3 g) sliced scallions

Remove the pizza dough from the refrigerator and allow it to come to room temperature while you cook the shrimp.

To make the shrimp scampi, place a large skillet over medium heat. Add the oil, shallots and lemon juice and cook for 1 minute. Add the garlic and white wine and cook for 30 seconds. Add the shrimp, lemon zest and a pinch of salt and cook until the shrimp are almost pink but not fully cooked, about 2 minutes. Remove from the heat and season with pepper. Set aside until needed.

If you have a pizza stone, place it in the oven prior to preheating. You can also use a preheated baker's pan. Or a neat trick is to use a preheated cast iron skillet, turn it over and the 12-inch (30-cm)-round bottom is a perfect replacement for a pizza stone. Preheat the oven to 500°F (260°C).

To make the pizza, flour a pizza peel or a clean work surface and stretch the dough out to approximately 12 inches (30 cm). Add the shrimp with its sauce on top, followed by the mozzarella cubes and the shredded mozzarella. Sprinkle the top with the scallions. Use the peel to transfer the pizza to the stone or pan in the oven. Or carefully remove the pan and use a metal spatula, or better yet a wide fish spatula, to move the pizza to the pan and return it to the oven.

Bake until the cheese has melted and the edges are golden brown, about 10 minutes. Slice and serve.

PEPPERONI PIZZA MAC & CHEESE

Flip 'N Toss, West Village, New York

Chef-owner David Thual makes the craziest burgers and extra-cheesy mac-and-cheese creations, which is why we love his spot in the West Village so much (see the Shrimp Big Mac 'n' Cheese Burger on page 41). This mac and cheese is anything but ordinary as it marries two of our favorite foods into something we just can't get enough of—and it has five kinds of cheese! "I wanted to take a dish that was the very definition of New York City—pizza—and give it a completely new spin," says Thual. "Not only do you get to try a different version of the classic New York slice, but you also get an incredible cheese pull for the 'Gram and a real satisfying meal for an affordable price."

SERVES 2 •

2 cloves garlic, unpeeled

2 medium shallots, unpeeled

1 tbsp (15 ml) extra-virgin olive oil

2 tbsp (36 g) salt

2 cups (230 g) uncooked elbow macaroni

3 cups (720 ml) heavy cream

½ cup (57 g) shredded yellow cheddar cheese

½ cup (56 g) shredded pepper jack cheese

1 tsp fresh thyme leaves

Kosher salt

Black pepper

3 tbsp (45 ml) pizza sauce

¼ cup (28 g) shredded Monterey jack cheese

¼ cup (28 g) shredded white cheddar cheese

15 slices pepperoni

¼ cup (28 g) small-diced fresh mozzarella cheese

¼ cup (10 g) chopped fresh basil

Preheat the oven to 350°F (175°C).

Place the whole unpeeled garlic cloves and shallots on a small piece of aluminum foil, drizzle with the olive oil, wrap them up in the foil and roast in the oven for 30 minutes. Remove and let cool a bit, then peel them. Keep the oven on—you'll use it to bake the pasta.

While they're roasting, add the salt to a large pot of water and bring to a boil over high heat. Add the macaroni and cook until al dente, about 1 minute less than the package directions. Drain and set aside.

In a large saucepan over medium heat, add the cream and yellow cheddar and pepper jack cheeses, stirring to combine. When the cheese has melted, add the thyme, peeled roasted garlic and peeled roasted shallots, mashing them with a fork to incorporate into the sauce. Season to taste with kosher salt and pepper. Add the cooked macaroni and pizza sauce and stir to combine. Add the Monterey jack and white cheddar cheeses and stir to combine.

Pour the mixture into an oven-safe round casserole dish, top with the pepperoni and mozzarella, and bake for 5 minutes. Remove from the oven and allow to cool for 5 minutes before topping with fresh basil and serving.

LOBSTER BURRATA PASTA

Bella Gioia, Park Slope, Brooklyn

Located in the Park Slope neighborhood of Brooklyn, Bella Gioia is a rustic and charming restaurant specializing in Sicilian comfort foods. This dish combines our twin loves of seafood and mac and cheese into one decadent dish. "Pasta, lobster and burrata—what's not to like about it?" says chef-owner Nico Daniele. The addition of sweet lobster meat ups the elegance by a factor of ten, while the use of burrata creates a super-creamy sauce. We recommend using fresh-cooked lobster, but frozen and thawed cooked lobster works well too as long as you cook most of the water out of it.

SERVES 1 •

2 tbsp (28 g) kosher salt, plus more for seasoning

5 oz (⅓ lb [142 g]) thick spaghetti, such as tagliolini

½ cup (120 ml) extra-virgin olive oil, plus more for garnish

Pinch of crushed red pepper flakes

2 cloves garlic, minced

1 lobster tail, cooked, shelled and cut into 1-inch (2.5-cm) pieces

1 lobster claw, cooked, shelled and cut into 1-inch (2.5-cm) pieces

¼ cup (60 ml) white wine

1 cup (240 ml) fish or lobster stock

1 tbsp (14 g) butter

Zest of 1 lemon

Black pepper

1 (4-oz [113-g]) ball burrata

½ tbsp (2 g) chopped fresh parsley

Add the kosher salt to a large pot of water and bring to a boil over high heat. Add the pasta and cook until al dente, about 1 minute less than the package instructions. Scoop out and reserve 1 cup (240 ml) of the pasta water before draining the pasta.

In a large skillet over medium heat, add the olive oil and red pepper flakes and cook for 30 seconds. Add the garlic and cook until it's lightly browned and fragrant, about 1 minute. Add the cooked lobster and heat until the seafood has stopped releasing liquid, 2 to 5 minutes, depending on whether the meat was frozen. Add the white wine and cook for 30 seconds. Add the fish stock and cook until it's reduced by half, about 2 minutes. Add the butter, pasta and reserved pasta water and cook for 1 minute, stirring the pasta into the sauce. Remove from the heat and stir in the lemon zest. Taste and adjust the seasoning, adding salt and pepper as needed.

Transfer to a plate, top with the burrata, season with pepper, drizzle with olive oil and garnish with the parsley.

CHAPTER 4

KEEPIN' IT SAUCY

WACKY WINGS

Okay, here's the moment we've all been waiting for . . . WANGZZZZ! They are Rebecca's favorite food group and are even the subject of one of our YouTube channel series called *Wings with M'Wife*. So, needless to say, we are very serious about our chicken wings and where to find the best of the best. From *super* spicy to sticky sweet, wings of all stripes are our obsession. We have zero limits when it comes to the heat, flavor and sauce.

This chapter offers a plethora of wacky flavors, from Mango Habanero Bacon (page 84) to Smoky Manhattan (page 87). And it doesn't stop there. Get ready for one of our all-time favorite wing setups from Brooklyn, where the Buffalo drums and flappers come with a creamy side of Alabama white sauce (page 81).

Just to throw you guys for a double loop, we then travel into uncharted territory by presenting a pair of nonpoultry wing-like recipes that were too good not to share—General Tso's Pig Wings (page 88) and Charred Pork Ribs (page 91)— both unearthed in Williamsburg, Brooklyn.

Oh, and if you think you can handle the heat, head straight to the Firecracker Wings recipe (page 78), which is as radioactive as the name suggests. We tried to make sure all bases were covered!

FIRECRACKER WINGS

International Wings Factory, Upper East Side, New York

We asked chef-owner Deepak Ballaney to bring the heat, and did he ever! These addictive munchies are called Firecracker Wings for good reason—and that reason is the infamous Carolina reaper chili (20 of them, to be precise). Despite the chili pepper's reputation as one of the hottest in the world, this recipe offers more of a creeper heat that builds and builds, stopping just short of melt-your-face-off. But there's more to this complex sauce than blinding heat, thanks to sweet roasted peppers and earthy dark chocolate. A tip from the chef: Wear gloves when handling the hot peppers. Added bonus: This recipe makes lots of extra sauce for you to store in the fridge and use later!

MAKES 24 WINGS •

CHILI SAUCE

20 dried Carolina reaper chilies

4 cups (960 ml) warm water

1½ cups (360 ml) Frank's RedHot® cayenne pepper sauce

½ cup (120 ml) scotch bonnet pepper hot sauce

½ cup (120 ml) extra-virgin olive oil, divided

½ cup (75 g) chopped roasted red bell peppers

1 tbsp (16 g) tomato paste

1 tbsp (7 g) smoked paprika

½ tbsp (7 g) kosher salt

1 tbsp (8 g) garlic powder

½ tsp onion powder

1 tbsp (5 g) unsweetened dark cocoa powder

½ cup (120 ml) honey

Rehydrate the dried chilies by placing them in a large bowl with the warm water. Leave at room temperature for 24 hours and then refrigerate for 24 hours. Drain the rehydrated chilies, reserving the liquid.

In a large bowl, add the reserved liquid along with the Frank's RedHot and scotch bonnet hot sauces. Set aside.

In a large saucepan over medium-high heat, add ¼ cup (60 ml) of the oil and the drained chilies, roasted red peppers, tomato paste and paprika and bring to a simmer. Add the Frank's RedHot liquid mixture, bring it to a boil and reduce the heat to medium-low. Simmer until the liquid has reduced by half, about 10 minutes. Transfer to a blender or food processor and process until the mixture is smooth, making sure to scrape down the sides a few times. Add the salt, garlic powder, onion powder, cocoa powder and remaining ¼ cup (60 ml) of oil and pulse to blend. Strain the chili sauce through a cheesecloth or fine strainer, discarding or reserving the solids for another use. Return the liquid to the saucepan, bring to a boil and add the honey. Bottle and store in the refrigerator until needed.

(continued)

BRINE

2 tbsp (28 g) kosher salt

2 tbsp (17 g) chopped garlic

24 whole chicken wings, split

GARNISH

1 tbsp (8 g) confectioners' sugar

2 scallions, sliced

FIRECRACKER WINGS (CONT.)

In a large pot over high heat, add 1½ gallons (5.7 L) of water and the salt and garlic. Bring to a boil and simmer until it's reduced by one-third, about 15 minutes. Cool, add the chicken wings, cover and refrigerate overnight.

When you're ready to cook, place the pot with the brine and chicken wings over high heat and bring to a simmer. Simmer for 7 minutes. Remove the wings to a paper towel–lined platter to drain.

Preheat the oven to 400°F (205°C).

Arrange the chicken wings in a single layer on a sheet pan and roast until the meat reaches an internal temperature of 165°F (75°C), about 20 minutes. Transfer to a large bowl, add the chili sauce to taste and toss to combine. Sprinkle with the confectioners' sugar and scallions, and serve.

GRILLED BBQ BUFFALO WINGS WITH ALABAMA WHITE SAUCE

Pig Beach, Gowanus, Brooklyn

"Low and slow wins the race!" declares Chef Matt Abdoo of Pig Beach. This barbecue-themed beer garden in Brooklyn is one of our all-time favorite summertime hangs because it is people-friendly, dog-friendly and smells like a little bit of heaven thanks to the grills and smokers that keep guests well fed. There are a lot of homemade elements to this recipe, we know, but we think the results are worth the effort. If you have never had Alabama White Sauce, prepare to be blown away. It is a million times more interesting than the same-old blue cheese or ranch dipping sauce that normally accompanies wings. "Alabama White is the perfect dunk for the wings," says the chef.

SERVES 1 •

ALABAMA WHITE SAUCE

½ cup (120 ml) mayonnaise

2 tsp (10 ml) apple cider vinegar

1 tsp apple juice

1 tsp lemon juice

½ tsp grated horseradish

⅓ tsp black pepper

2 tsp (10 g) sugar

¼ tsp kosher salt

½ tsp dry barbecue seasoning mix

POULTRY SEASONING

1 tsp kosher salt

¼ tsp black pepper

¼ tsp sugar

1 tsp sweet paprika

¼ tsp smoked paprika

¼ tsp granulated onion

¼ tsp granulated garlic

Pinch of dried thyme

To make the Alabama white sauce, place the mayonnaise, apple cider vinegar, apple juice, lemon juice, horseradish, pepper, sugar, salt and barbecue seasoning in a medium bowl and whisk to combine. Cover and refrigerate overnight.

To make the poultry seasoning, place the salt, pepper, sugar, sweet paprika, smoked paprika, granulated onion, granulated garlic and thyme in a small bowl and stir to combine. Set aside until needed.

(continued)

VINEGAR BBQ SAUCE

1 tbsp (15 ml) white vinegar

1½ tsp (8 ml) apple juice

1½ tsp (8 ml) ketchup

½ tsp dark brown sugar

¼ tsp kosher salt

⅛ tsp black pepper

⅛ tsp crushed red pepper flakes

⅛ tsp chili powder

BUFFALO WING SAUCE

2 tbsp (28 g) butter

1 tbsp (15 ml) Frank's RedHot cayenne pepper sauce

2 tbsp (30 ml) Vinegar BBQ Sauce

ASSEMBLY

1 lb (454 g) whole chicken wings

1 tbsp (7 g) Poultry Seasoning

¼ cup (60 ml) Buffalo Wing Sauce

Carrot and celery sticks, for serving

GRILLED BBQ BUFFALO WINGS WITH ALABAMA WHITE SAUCE (CONT.)

To make the vinegar BBQ sauce, place the white vinegar, apple juice, ketchup, brown sugar, salt, black pepper, red pepper flakes and chili powder in a nonreactive container and whisk to combine. Set aside until needed.

To make the Buffalo wing sauce, place the butter in a small saucepan over medium heat to melt. Add the Frank's RedHot and vinegar BBQ sauce and whisk to combine. Cover and refrigerate until needed.

Pat the chicken wings dry with paper towels. Toss with the poultry seasoning and let sit for 15 minutes.

Meanwhile, preheat a gas or charcoal grill to medium-low heat. Place the wings on an upper rack, cover and cook until the meat reaches an internal temperature of 150°F (65°C), about 15 minutes. Increase the heat to medium-high and grill the wings until they have a nice char on all sides and the meat reaches an internal temperature of 165°F (75°C), about 1 minute per side.

Remove the chicken wings to a large mixing bowl, add the Buffalo wing sauce and toss to coat. Serve with Alabama white sauce, carrots and celery.

CHEF'S NOTE: If you don't have outdoor space to grill, all of the steps can be mirrored for a home oven set at 250°F (120°C). Add 1 teaspoon of smoked paprika when you toss the wings with the poultry seasoning to get that smoky flavor. Once the wings are fully cooked through (about 3 hours low and slow), finish them in a hot oven (400°F [205°C]) for 5 to 10 minutes to get the skin crispy. Then toss in the sauce and serve.

MANGO HABANERO BACON WINGS

Morgan's Brooklyn Barbecue, Flatbush, Brooklyn

For this recipe, we stop by Morgan's Brooklyn Barbecue, where the kitchen serves chicken wings like no other. (Spoiler alert: They are sprinkled with bacon.) Cenobio Canalizo, the chef at Morgan's, has come up with some really, really cool over-the-top barbecue recipes, and this is no exception. Get ready to get your hands sticky! Warning: The Mango Habanero Sauce packs some serious heat.

MAKES 12 WINGS •

BRINE

½ cup (100 g) granulated sugar

¼ cup (56 g) kosher salt

¼ cup (60 ml) canola oil

12 jumbo whole chicken wings

**MANGO HABANERO SAUCE
(enough for 2 servings)**

2 tsp (10 ml) extra-virgin olive oil

2 tbsp (20 g) chopped white onion

⅔ cup (160 ml) rice vinegar

11 oz (302 g) fresh mango flesh

12 oz (340 g) mango purée
(⅓ of a 2.2-lb [998-g] tub)

⅓ cup (80 ml) sweet chili sauce

1 fresh habanero pepper, seeded

⅓ tsp sweet paprika

2 tsp (10 g) kosher salt

2 tsp (10 g) butter

1 cup (240 ml) water

ASSEMBLY

1½ tsp (7 g) kosher salt

1½ tsp (3 g) black pepper

¾ tsp Lawry's® Seasoned Salt

⅓ lb (151 g) sliced bacon

4 cups (960 ml) vegetable oil

Celery sticks, for serving

To brine the chicken, place the sugar, salt, oil and 1 gallon (3.8 L) of cold water in a large sealable container and stir to dissolve the sugar and salt. Add the chicken wings, cover and refrigerate overnight.

To make the mango habanero sauce, place a large saucepan over medium-high heat, add the oil and onion, and cook until the onion is lightly browned, about 2 minutes. Add the rice vinegar and cook until it's reduced by half, about 5 minutes. Add the mango, mango purée, sweet chili sauce, habanero pepper, paprika, salt, butter and water and bring to a boil. Reduce the heat to low and simmer for 1 hour. Transfer to a blender or food processor and process until smooth, making sure to scrape down the sides a few times. Set aside until needed.

Prepare and preheat a smoker to 175°F (80°C).

Remove the chicken wings from the brine and drain. Discard the brine. In a large bowl, add the wings, salt, pepper and Lawry's Seasoned Salt and toss to coat. Place the wings in the smoker for 3 hours.

Meanwhile, preheat the oven to 350°F (175°C). Arrange the bacon on a sheet pan and cook until it's crispy, about 15 minutes. When the bacon is cool enough to handle, chop it into small pieces and set aside.

In a tabletop fryer or large, heavy pot over medium-high heat, add the oil. Heat it to 350°F (175°C). In batches, carefully add the smoked chicken wings to the hot oil and fry until they're golden brown, about 8 minutes per batch. Transfer the wings to a paper towel–lined plate to drain.

Immediately toss with the mango habanero sauce and bacon and serve with celery sticks.

CHEF'S NOTE: If you don't have a smoker, you can bake the wings in the oven for 45 minutes at 375°F (190°C), then just finish them in the fryer. Of course, you won't get the same smoky flavor but they will still taste great.

SMOKY MANHATTAN WINGS
Holy Ground NYC, Multiple Locations, New York

Every Sunday during football season, Chef Franco Vlasic and his friends get together to watch the Giants play. "At the time I came up with this recipe, there was only one restaurant in my neighborhood that delivered decent wings," he explains. "However, they were horrible in terms of getting the food there on time." So Vlasic took matters into his own hands. The key here, he says, is to grill the wings until they get really dark, almost burnt. "That's just the sugar in the rub caramelizing. Wait till the skin starts to bubble a little for perfect wings."

MAKES 50 WINGS ●

25 whole chicken wings, split

¾ cup (about 80 g) your favorite spice blend (see Chef's Notes)

2 tbsp (28 g) butter (or butter substitute)

2 cups (480 ml) Frank's RedHot cayenne pepper sauce

In a large mixing bowl, add the wings and the spice blend and toss to coat. Set aside while you preheat the grill.

Preheat a gas or charcoal grill to medium-high heat. Toss a few handfuls of wood chips or chunks onto the hot coals (or, for gas grills, wrap some wood chips in foil, poke a few holes in the pouch and toss it right on the grill grate), close the lid and wait a few minutes for the smoke to start.

Place the chicken on the grill, close the lid and cook until the wings release from the grates easily, about 10 minutes. Flip the wings, cover and continue cooking until the skin is crispy and begins to bubble, about 10 minutes.

Meanwhile, melt the butter in a medium saucepan over medium heat. Add the Frank's RedHot sauce and bring to a low simmer. Turn off the heat.

When the wings are done, toss them in the warm sauce and serve.

CHEF'S NOTES: Choose a spice blend that is sweet, smoky and spicy. Key ingredients to look for would be brown sugar, chili powder, salt and pepper.

If you don't have an outdoor grill, you can make a makeshift smoker out of your oven by using wood chips, a baking tray, a roasting rack and some foil. Soak some wood chips in a bowl of water, then lay them out on the baking tray. Place the roasting rack in the tray so that there's some space between the bottom of the rack and the chips. Put the wings on the rack and cover the whole thing with foil like a giant package. Let that cook at 250°F (120°C) for about 45 minutes. Then you'll want to finish the wings on a grill pan set over high heat on the stovetop to give them some nice char.

GENERAL TSO'S PIG WINGS
Wing Jawn, Williamsburg, Brooklyn

Located in Kilo Bravo Bar in Williamsburg, Brooklyn, Wing Jawn is a collaboration between Kate Buenaflor Dillon and Dave and Stella Fedoroff, the chefs who also shared recipes for Philly Cheesesteak (page 23) and Bronson Fries (page 125). While we adore chicken wings, this recipe stood out for us because they are PORK WINGS. Well, they're not really wings, but rather pork shanks that are slow cooked and then deep fried, leaving them crispy *and* fall-off-the-bone tender. The sticky, sweet and spicy General Tso sauce is the perfect finish for these unique "wings."

MAKES 4 PIG WINGS ●

1 small yellow onion, roughly chopped

2 cloves garlic, smashed

4 bone-in pork shanks (about 1½ lbs [680 g] total)

Kosher salt

Black pepper

1½ cups (360 ml) low-sodium chicken broth, divided

GENERAL TSO SAUCE

3 tbsp (45 ml) rice vinegar

¼ cup (60 ml) low-sodium soy sauce

2 tbsp (30 ml) hoisin sauce

3 tbsp (45 g) white sugar

3 tbsp (42 g) brown sugar

1 tsp grated fresh ginger

½ tsp garlic powder

¼ tsp crushed red pepper flakes

1 tbsp (8 g) cornstarch

4 cups (960 ml) vegetable oil

2 scallions, sliced

1 tbsp (9 g) sesame seeds

In a slow cooker, add the onion, garlic and pork shanks and season with salt and pepper. Add 1 cup (240 ml) of chicken broth, cover and cook on high for 3½ hours.

About 15 minutes before the pork is done cooking, make the General Tso sauce. In a medium saucepan over medium heat, add the rice vinegar, soy sauce, hoisin sauce, white sugar, brown sugar, ginger, garlic powder, red pepper flakes, cornstarch and remaining ½ cup (120 ml) of chicken broth and whisk to combine. Bring to a simmer and cook until the mixture begins to thicken, about 5 minutes. Remove from the heat and cover to keep warm.

Remove the pork shanks from the slow cooker. Discard the broth.

In a tabletop fryer or large, heavy pot over medium-high heat, add the oil. Heat to 350°F (175°C).

Carefully add the pork shanks to the hot oil and fry until crispy, about 4 minutes. Transfer to a paper towel–lined plate to drain. Toss the wings in the General Tso sauce, garnish with the scallions and sesame seeds, and serve.

CHARRED PORK RIBS
Glaze Teriyaki, Multiple Locations, New York

In addition to the epic chicken wings in this chapter, we had to include one of our favorite untraditional wing-like discoveries that will have you licking your fingers. What elevates this recipe above other rib-cooking methods is the combination of slow-roasting and high-heat grilling, which produces an extra-crispy exterior surrounding fall-off-the-bone meaty goodness. The crowning glory is the hoisin barbecue sauce—an irresistible sweet and tangy glaze with a touch of heat. This recipe should leave you with extra sauce to serve on the side with the hot ribs.

MAKES 1 RACK OF RIBS •

HOISIN BARBECUE SAUCE
¼ lb (113 g) bacon, diced

2 cups (320 g) diced yellow onion

1½ tbsp (9 g) chopped fresh ginger

1⅓ cups (320 ml) white vinegar

½ cup (110 g) light brown sugar

3⅓ cups (800 ml) ketchup

⅓ cup (80 ml) soy sauce

¼ cup (60 ml) yellow mustard

1 tbsp (17 g) chipotle peppers in adobo sauce

1 cup (240 ml) hoisin sauce

1 tbsp (9 g) whole black peppercorns

PORK RIBS
1 rack pork spare ribs

Kosher salt

Black pepper

2 cups (480 ml) water

1 cup (200 g) uncooked white rice, rinsed

1 tbsp (9 g) sesame seeds

To make the hoisin barbecue sauce, place a large saucepan over medium-high heat and add the bacon. Cook, stirring occasionally, until the bacon is crispy, about 8 minutes. Add the onion and ginger and cook until they're soft, about 3 minutes. Add the white vinegar and bring to a simmer. Add the brown sugar, ketchup, soy sauce, mustard, chipotle peppers in adobo sauce, hoisin sauce and peppercorns and simmer, uncovered, for 2 hours. Carefully transfer the mixture to the bowl of a blender or food processor and process until smooth. Cover and refrigerate until needed.

For the ribs, preheat the oven to 325°F (165°C).

Liberally season both sides of the ribs with salt and pepper. Wrap in foil, place on a sheet pan and bake for 3 hours, removing the foil for the last 10 minutes. When the ribs are cool enough to handle, cut between the bones to get individual ribs.

While the ribs are cooking, place a medium saucepan over medium-high heat. Add the water and a pinch of salt and bring to a boil. Add the rice, reduce the heat to low, cover and cook until the rice has fully absorbed the liquid, about 20 minutes.

Preheat a gas or charcoal grill or a stovetop grill pan to high heat. Add the ribs and liberally brush them with the hoisin barbecue sauce. Grill about 2 to 3 minutes, turn, liberally brush again and cook until all sides are well caramelized but not burnt, about 2 to 3 minutes more.

To serve, place the ribs on the steamed rice and sprinkle with the sesame seeds.

CHEF'S NOTE: We finish the ribs on the grill pan with the hoisin barbecue sauce just to create a little char. This also loosens the proteins and creates the fall-off-the-bone finished product.

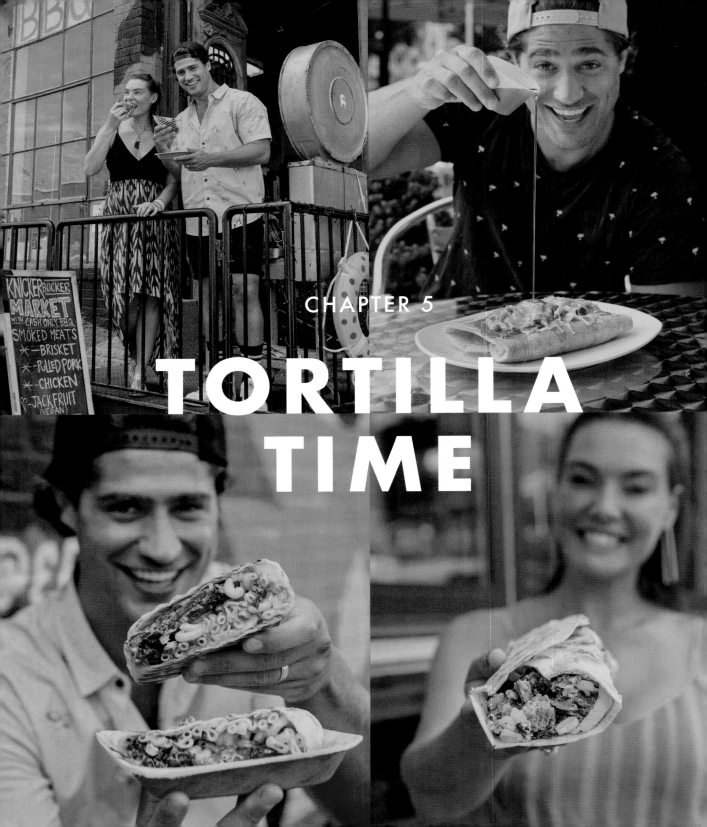

CHAPTER 5

TORTILLA TIME

TACO VIBES AND BADASS BURRITOS

Super-stuffed burritos that can barely contain their fillings and crisp-edged quesadillas that are almost too heavy to lift . . . that is our JAM! We tracked down some of the most decadent ingredients that definitely bring the WOW factor to life. We even added a couple of special surprises, including a seriously addictive kettle queso (page 94) to dip, dunk and plunge these bad-boy burritos into.

Want a serious twist on the classic tortilla shell? Then behold the pancake burrito (page 103)! Okay, we've given away too much already. Just flip the pages yourself to experience the rest.

In this chapter, we travel to Brooklyn, Chinatown, Astoria, the Lower East Side, the Upper East Side and the East Village, so load up those MetroCards and prepare to swipe your way to ecstasy.

STEAK BURRITO WITH KETTLE QUESO

Conmigo, Upper East Side, New York

Chef Billy Demiris was in California when he stumbled upon the secret ingredient that would forever change his Mexican cooking. "I was on my way to San Diego when my friend and I decided to stop at some food truck in the middle of nowhere," the chef recalls. "As we were standing there inhaling our food, I got to talking with the owner and found out about the special ingredient he was using in all his dishes: achiote paste." Demiris, who describes achiote as earthy, peppery and slightly bitter, warns that "a little achiote paste goes a long way," so be light-handed. This dish normally isn't sold as a burrito and queso combo, but our love of melty cheese and meat had us at *hello*. We ordered this thick, juicy burrito and proceeded to deep-dunk it into the queso. Still not sorry.

MAKES 4 BURRITOS •

GUACAMOLE

2 avocados, halved and pitted

¼ cup (40 g) diced white onion

¼ cup (4 g) chopped fresh cilantro

Juice of 1 lime

Kosher salt

STEAK

¼ cup (60 ml) soy sauce

1 tbsp (16 g) achiote paste

1½ lbs (680 g) boneless short rib, cut into ¼-inch (6-mm) slices

RICE

1 tbsp (15 ml) canola oil

2 cloves garlic, minced

1 cup (200 g) uncooked long-grain rice

2 cups (480 ml) chicken broth

2 tsp (11 g) achiote paste

1 plum tomato, puréed

Kosher salt

Black pepper

To make the guacamole, use a spoon to scoop the flesh from the avocados and place it in a medium bowl. Mash with a fork until it's smooth. Add the onion, cilantro and lime juice and stir to combine. Season to taste with salt. Cover and refrigerate until needed.

Get the steak marinating. In a medium bowl, add the soy sauce and achiote paste and stir to combine. Add the short rib, toss to coat and set aside for at least 10 minutes.

To make the rice, in a large saucepan over medium heat, add the oil and garlic and cook until fragrant, about 1 minute. Add the rice and cook for 1 minute, stirring constantly. Add the broth and bring to a simmer. Add the achiote paste and tomato, stir, cover and cook until the rice has fully absorbed the liquid, about 20 minutes. Season to taste with salt and pepper. Cover and keep warm.

(continued)

KETTLE QUESO

3 cups (336 g) shredded Oaxaca or mozzarella cheese

2 cups (226 g) shredded cheddar cheese

½ cup (120 ml) whole milk

¼ cup (60 ml) puréed chipotle peppers in adobo sauce

Kosher salt

Black pepper

ASSEMBLY

4 flour tortillas

1 (15.5-oz [439-g]) can black beans, drained

2 cups (480 ml) sour cream

STEAK BURRITO WITH KETTLE QUESO (CONT.)

To make the kettle queso, in a medium bowl, add the Oaxaca and cheddar cheeses and toss to combine. In a large nonstick saucepan over low heat, add the milk. When it's warm, begin adding the cheese ½ cup (57 g) at a time, stirring constantly. Wait until the cheese has fully melted before adding the next handful. When all the cheese has been added and has melted, add the chipotle peppers in adobo sauce and mix well. Season to taste with salt and pepper. Remove from the heat and transfer to an oven-safe crock. Preheat the broiler to high. Place the queso under the broiler until the cheese is lightly browned. Remove and cover to keep warm.

Remove the steak from the marinade, allowing the excess to drip off. Discard the marinade. Place a large skillet over medium-high heat. Add the steak and cook, stirring occasionally, until the meat is completely browned and cooked through, about 8 minutes. Remove from the pan and cover to keep warm.

To the now-empty skillet over medium-high heat, warm the tortillas on both sides in batches. To assemble the burritos, divide the meat, rice, beans, guacamole and sour cream evenly among the 4 tortillas and serve with kettle queso.

LOADED CARNE ASADA QUESADILLAS

Dos Toros Taqueria, Multiple Locations, New York

Dos Toros Taqueria is one of our favorite fast-casual Mexican joints. With items that range from Mission-style burritos and cheesy quesadillas to carnitas-topped nachos, it's almost impossible to pull the trigger. These Loaded Carne Asada Quesadillas are a nod to the foods that cofounders Leo and Oliver Kremer enjoyed as kids living on the West Coast. "This quesadilla was one of our favorite meals growing up," they say. "When we moved to the East Coast, we couldn't find anything like it. It's a little messy, but that's part of the fun." They caution against cooking the skirt steak past medium-rare, or else it gets tough and chewy.

MAKES 4 QUESADILLAS •

GUACAMOLE

6 avocados, pitted and diced

1½ tsp (7 g) kosher salt

Juice of 2 limes

½ small red onion, diced

¼ cup (4 g) chopped fresh cilantro

TOMATO SALSA

6 Roma tomatoes, diced

1½ small red onions, diced

1 cup (16 g) chopped fresh cilantro

¼ cup (60 ml) lime juice

1 tbsp (14 g) kosher salt

SALSA VERDE HOT SAUCE

5 whole jalapeño peppers, stems removed

9 whole tomatillos, husks removed

¼ cup (40 g) diced yellow onion

6 cloves garlic

2 tsp (10 g) kosher salt

2 cups (480 ml) water

To make the guacamole, place the avocados and salt in medium bowl and lightly mash with a fork, making sure to leave it a little chunky. Add the lime juice, red onion and cilantro, and mix gently to combine. Cover and refrigerate until needed.

To make the tomato salsa, place the tomatoes, onions, cilantro, lime juice and salt in a medium bowl and mix to combine. Cover and refrigerate until needed.

To make the salsa verde hot sauce, preheat a gas or charcoal grill or a stovetop grill pan to medium-high heat and grill the jalapeños until all sides are lightly charred, about 8 minutes total. In a medium saucepan over medium heat, add the grilled jalapeños, tomatillos, onion, garlic, salt and water and cook until the vegetables are very soft, about 30 minutes. Transfer to a blender or food processor and process until smooth, making sure to scrape down the sides a few times. Set aside until needed.

(continued)

QUESADILLAS

1 lb (454 g) skirt steak

½ tsp sweet paprika

Kosher salt

Black pepper

Vegetable oil

4 (13-inch [33-cm]) flour tortillas

2 cups (224 g) shredded Monterey jack cheese

OPTIONAL ADD-INS

Corn

Black beans

Sour cream

LOADED CARNE ASADA QUESADILLAS (CONT.)

To cook the meat, preheat a gas or charcoal grill or a stovetop grill pan to high heat. Season both sides of the steak with paprika, salt and pepper. Drizzle both sides with oil and place the meat on the grill. Cook until a nice crust forms on the bottom, about 3 minutes. Flip and cook the other side until a nice crust forms, about 3 minutes. Remove from the heat, cover and let rest for 5 minutes. Thinly slice the steak against the grain, cover and set aside.

Place a large skillet over medium-high heat. Add a drizzle of vegetable oil followed by 1 tortilla. Top with ½ cup (56 g) of shredded cheese and cook until the tortilla turns golden brown and the cheese begins to melt, about 2 minutes. Remove the tortilla to a plate and arrange one-quarter of the meat in the center. Top with ¼ cup (65 g) of tomato salsa, ¼ cup (58 g) of guacamole and salsa verde hot sauce to taste. Add any optional add-ins you'd like. Fold the edges of the tortilla over the center to form a rectangle. Repeat the process with the remaining 3 tortillas.

BULGOGI CHEESESTEAK TACOS

SET L.E.S., Lower East Side, New York

At SET L.E.S. on the Lower East Side (LES) of Manhattan, owner Mikey Tang has dreamed up a gourmet pub grub menu that spans many culinary genres. These amazing tacos, for example, combine the joys of Korean bulgogi with the familiar thrills of Mexican tacos. If you haven't tried it, bulgogi is thinly sliced steak marinated in a sticky and delicious sweet-salty-garlicky glaze. The final garnish of sriracha mayo adds a creamy tang to each meaty, cheesy bite.

MAKES 4 TACOS •

2 cloves garlic, minced

¼-inch (6-mm) piece fresh ginger, grated

3 tbsp (45 ml) light soy sauce

1½ tsp (8 ml) sesame oil

1½ tbsp (23 g) sugar

Kosher salt

Black pepper

¾ lb (340 g) ribeye steak, very thinly sliced against the grain

1 tbsp (15 ml) vegetable oil

1 large onion, thinly sliced

1 red bell pepper, seeded and thinly sliced

1 green bell pepper, seeded and thinly sliced

¼ cup (60 ml) sriracha sauce

¼ cup (60 ml) mayonnaise

2 cups (225 g) shredded mozzarella, sharp cheddar, provolone or American cheese

4 flour tortillas

Pico de gallo

Sliced scallions

In a medium bowl, add the garlic, ginger, soy sauce, sesame oil, sugar and a pinch of salt and pepper and whisk to combine. Add the sliced beef, toss to combine, cover and refrigerate for 30 minutes.

In a large skillet over medium heat, add the oil, onion and red and green bell peppers. Cook, stirring occasionally, until the vegetables are well caramelized, about 10 minutes. Remove from the heat.

To make the sriracha mayo, in a small bowl stir together the sriracha sauce and mayonnaise until they are evenly combined. Set aside.

Preheat a grill pan or a large skillet over medium-high heat. Remove the beef from the marinade, allowing the excess to drip off. Discard the marinade. Working in batches so as not to crowd the pan, add the beef slices and cook until crisp, about 1 minute per side. As the slices are done, remove them to a plate.

Preheat the broiler to medium-high.

Divide the meat into four equal portions and arrange it in piles on a sheet pan. Divide the sautéed vegetables and then the cheese equally among the four piles. Place the sheet pan under the broiler to melt the cheese.

When the cheese has melted, transfer the piles to the tortillas and dress with the sriracha mayo, pico de gallo and scallions.

PANCAKE BURRITO

Mom's Kitchen & Bar, Astoria, Queens

Owner Rob Williamson describes this dish as "the best of all things breakfast wrapped into one"—and he couldn't be more accurate. This dish literally rolls up all of our favorite breakfast foods into one of the craziest and most insanely delicious breakfast dishes out there. Yes, it is a pancake stuffed with bacon, sausage, scrambled eggs and cheese, rolled up into a magical breakfast burrito. We love to drizzle our favorite hot sauce on top, but if you just want to go the sweet maple syrup route, you do you.

MAKES 1 BURRITO •

1 cup (240 ml) buttermilk

½ cup (120 ml) water

1½ cups (180 g) your favorite pancake mix

Kosher salt

1 tsp vegetable oil

3 slices bacon

1 pork and sage sausage link

2 eggs

1 tsp mascarpone cheese, at room temperature

2 tsp (3 g) chopped chives, divided

1 cup (113 g) shredded cheddar cheese (white, yellow or a mix), divided

¼ cup (60 ml) pure maple syrup

To make the pancake batter, in a large bowl, add the buttermilk and water. Add the pancake mix and a pinch of salt and whisk to combine, making sure to not overwork the batter. Set aside.

Preheat the oven to 350°F (175°C).

Place a large skillet or griddle over medium heat. Add the oil, bacon and sausage and cook, turning once halfway through, until they're fully cooked and crispy, about 4 minutes per side for the bacon and 5 minutes per side for the sausage, or until the sausage reaches an internal temperature of 160°F (70°C). Transfer both to a paper towel–lined plate to drain. Discard all but 1 tablespoon (15 ml) of fat from the skillet. When the meat is cool enough to handle, roughly chop the bacon and sausage, making sure to keep them separate, and set aside until needed.

In a small bowl, add the eggs, mascarpone and 1 teaspoon of chives and whisk to combine. Add the eggs to the pan you cooked the bacon in, and cook, stirring occasionally, until they're cooked through, about 4 minutes. Transfer to a plate and cover to keep warm.

Ladle the pancake batter into the same pan in a large rectangular shape. When bubbles begin forming around the edges, arrange the scrambled eggs, sausage and ½ cup (57 g) of the cheddar cheese on top. When the bottom of the pancake turns golden brown (about 1½ to 2 minutes), use two spatulas to roll it from the long end into a burrito. Continue cooking until the batter is cooked through.

Transfer the pancake burrito to an oven-safe plate, top with the remaining ½ cup (56 g) cheese and all the bacon, and cook until the cheese is melted, about 5 minutes. Remove from the oven, top with maple syrup and the remaining 1 teaspoon of chives, and serve.

MPOSSIBLE™ TACOS

Diller, Lower East Side, New York

When most of us crave tacos, we typically think of chicken, beef, pork and maybe veggie-based fillings. Well, after trying this taco at Diller, we have to add Impossible™ plant-based meat to that list of delicious fillings (as crazy as that sounds). Owner Mike Garlick says his aim was to create a taco that appealed to all diets—referring of course to vegetarians. What he couldn't predict was how much it would appeal to unabashed carnivores like us. Warning: If you make these tacos for your friends and tell them they're meat-free, they will probably call you a liar.

MAKES 2 TACOS •

TACO SAUCE

¼ cup (37 g) pickled grape tomatoes

¼ cup (40 g) chopped white onion

2 cloves garlic

1 tbsp (1 g) chopped fresh cilantro

⅛ tsp ground cumin

½ tsp salt

½ tsp black pepper

A few dashes hot sauce (optional)

TACOS

½ lb (226 g) Impossible™ Burger blend

⅔ cup (106 g) chopped white onion

¼ tsp adobo seasoning

⅛ tsp smoked paprika

⅛ tsp dried oregano

Pinch of garlic powder

Pinch of black pepper

1 tbsp (15 ml) vegetable oil

4 (8-inch [20-cm]) corn tortillas

1 cup (113 g) shredded cheddar cheese

½ cup (35 g) shredded cabbage

¼ cup (4 g) chopped fresh cilantro

Pickled sweet peppers and pickled onions (optional)

To make the taco sauce, place the pickled tomatoes, onion, garlic, cilantro, cumin, salt and pepper in a blender or food processor and process until smooth, making sure to scrape down the sides a few times. Season with hot sauce to your taste (if using). Cover and refrigerate until needed.

To make the tacos, in a large bowl, combine the Impossible™ Burger blend, onion, adobo, paprika, oregano, garlic powder and pepper and mix to combine.

In a large skillet over medium-high heat, add the oil. When it's hot, add the Impossible™ meat mixture and cook, breaking apart the meat with a spatula, until it's completely brown, about 10 minutes. When it's done, remove to a plate and cover to keep warm.

Working in batches if necessary, warm the tortillas in a clean, dry skillet for 15 seconds per side.

To assemble the tacos, double up the tortillas and top each stack with some Impossible™ meat, cheddar cheese, cabbage, cilantro, taco sauce, pickled sweet peppers and onions (if using) and any other garnishes you like.

MAC WRAP WITH SMOKED PASTRAMI

Cash Only BBQ, Williamsburg, Brooklyn

We met chef-owner Corey Cash a few years back when someone told us about his incredible smoked pastrami. Needless to say, our lives were forever altered after that first visit. Since then, Cash Only BBQ has become one of our favorite under-the-radar spots. There's nothing fancy, over-the-top or showy about the restaurant. Instead, Cash's food does all the talking. As good as that smoked pastrami is on its own, something downright magical happens when it's folded into creamy mac and cheese, bundled up in a warm tortilla and griddled until golden brown and crispy. To make this recipe more home cook–friendly, Cash suggests picking up some smoked pastrami from your favorite neighborhood deli or barbecue joint.

MAKES 2 WRAPS

2 tbsp (36 g) salt

1 (1-lb [454-g]) box uncooked elbow macaroni

1½ cups (340 g) Velveeta® Cheese Sauce

2 tbsp (30 ml) Grey Poupon Dijon mustard

½ tbsp (8 ml) Cholula® Hot Sauce

1 tsp Worcestershire sauce

1 tbsp (7 g) smoked paprika

2 tsp (6 g) garlic powder

2 tsp (5 g) onion powder

1 tsp mustard powder

1 tsp chili powder

½ tsp ground cumin

¾ cup (85 g) shredded mild cheddar cheese, divided

2 (12-inch [30-cm]) flour tortillas

¾ lb (339 g) smoked pastrami, sliced

1 tbsp (15 ml) vegetable oil

Add the salt to a large pot of water and bring to a boil over high heat. Add the macaroni and cook until al dente, about 1 minute less than the package directions. Drain, rinse with cold water, drain again and set aside.

To make the macaroni-and-cheese sauce, place a large, heavy saucepan over medium-low heat and add the cheese sauce, mustard, hot sauce, Worcestershire sauce, paprika, garlic powder, onion powder, mustard powder, chili powder and cumin and whisk until smooth. Add the cooked macaroni and 6 tablespoons (43 g) of cheddar cheese and stir until the cheese is melted and the pasta is fully coated. Remove the pan from the heat.

To warm the tortillas, heat them in the microwave on high for 5 seconds. Alternatively, warm the tortillas in a clean, dry skillet over medium-high heat for 15 seconds per side.

Divide the macaroni-and-cheese sauce, pastrami and remaining 6 tablespoons (42 g) of shredded cheddar cheese evenly in the middle of each tortilla. Assemble the burritos by folding one side over the filling, the two ends over the first flap and the final side up over the whole thing to close.

Place a large skillet over medium-high heat and add the oil. When it's hot, add the burritos seam side down and cook until they're golden brown on the bottom, about 2 minutes. Flip and repeat with other side. When they're done, remove to a plate and let rest for 2 minutes before cutting each burrito in half and serving.

CHAPTER 6

FIRE STARTERS

NOT SO SMALL APPS

We're not going to lie: This chapter was very hard for us to narrow down. There are SO many over-the-top snacks and starters in NYC that we were going crazy trying to decide which ones to feature in this book. In the end, we selected the ones that we think will impress you the most and inspire you to get cooking at home.

Appetizers are like the opening act before the main event. They set the entire mood of the meal at a restaurant, house party or backyard barbecue. These recipes for anything-but-ordinary starters are sure to earn you the title of Party Host of the Year.

Crunchy deep-fried pickles (page 129), Slow-Cooked and Bourbon-Glazed Bacon (page 126), ridiculous French fries (page 125), nachos that will blow your mind (page 119), cauliflower like you've never seen it (page 112), mac-and-cheese balls that will forever ruin ordinary mac and cheese for you (page 111) and a burrata that oozes green pesto when sliced like a scene straight out of *Ghostbusters* (page 116)—seriously, it doesn't get much better than this!

Oh yeah, we also included a recipe for extra-cheesy, super-garlicky bread knots (page 115), so maybe save that one for a week when you don't plan on making out with anyone. LOL.

DYNAMITE MAC & CHEESE BALLS

Burger, Inc., Williamsburg, Brooklyn; Meatpacking District, New York

Since opening in 2016 at the Gansevoort Market in Chelsea, Burger, Inc., has become rightly famous for its gourmet hamburgers, spicy fried chicken sandwiches and totally loaded chili cheese fries. But by a mile, the most popular menu item at this burger bar is the Dynamite Mac & Cheese Balls, deep-fried poppers filled with hot pepper–spiked macaroni and cheese. On its own, Burger, Inc.'s second location in Williamsburg flies through about 500 orders per week, according to cofounder Randy Lee. These crispy, golden brown nuggets are filled with creamy, extra-cheesy mac and cheese that melts in your mouth.

MAKES 24 MAC & CHEESE BALLS

2 tbsp (28 g) + 1 tsp kosher salt, divided

½ lb (226 g) elbow macaroni

2 large jalapeño peppers, seeded and finely chopped

1 lb (454 g) shredded sharp cheddar cheese

1 (15-oz [425-g]) can nacho cheese sauce

½ tsp black pepper

½ tsp smoked paprika

½ tsp garlic powder

½ tsp onion powder

½ tsp dried thyme

1 cup (125 g) all-purpose flour

2 large eggs, beaten

2 cups (112 g) panko bread crumbs

2 quarts (1.9 L) vegetable or peanut oil

Add 2 tablespoons (28 g) of the kosher salt to a large pot of water and bring to a boil over high heat. Add the macaroni and cook until it's al dente, about 1 minute less than the package directions. Drain, rinse with cold water, drain again and set aside.

In a large mixing bowl, add the cooked pasta, jalapeños, cheddar cheese, nacho cheese sauce, the remaining teaspoon of kosher salt, pepper, paprika, garlic powder, onion powder and thyme. Stir well to combine. Cover and refrigerate for at least 2 hours or overnight.

When you're ready to cook, put the flour in a shallow bowl, put the eggs in a second shallow bowl and put the panko in a third shallow bowl.

Use an ice cream scoop to portion the chilled mac-and-cheese mixture into 24 balls. Working with one ball at a time, dredge it in the flour, making sure to evenly coat it. Roll the ball in the beaten eggs, allowing the excess to drip off. Finally, roll the ball in the panko, making sure to evenly coat it. Set it on a large sheet pan. Repeat with the remaining mac-and-cheese balls.

In tabletop fryer or a large, heavy pot over medium-high heat, add the oil. Heat to 350°F (175°C). Set a cooling rack on a large sheet pan.

Working in batches, carefully lower the mac-and-cheese balls into the hot oil and fry for 30 seconds. Use a slotted spoon to raise the balls out of the oil for 30 seconds, then return the balls to the oil for another 30 seconds. Raise the balls out of the oil for another 30 seconds. Finally, lower the balls back into the oil and fry until they're golden brown and the cheese starts to ooze out, about 2 minutes. Remove the balls to the cooling rack set on a sheet pan to drain. Repeat with the remaining mac-and-cheese balls. Serve hot, while the cheese is warm and melty.

KENTUCKY FRIED CAULIFLOWER WITH HOT HONEY

Silver Light Tavern, Williamsburg, Brooklyn

Until we stopped by the Silver Light Tavern, we had never heard of Kentucky Fried Cauliflower, so we definitely had to try it. Chef Matt Olley says he was inspired to come up with a vegan version of Kentucky fried chicken, and this dish was the result. Vegans, he reports, love it because it is not the same old grilled cauliflower steak or Buffalo-style cauliflower. We love it because of the hot honey dipping sauce, which adds the perfect amount of sweet heat.

SERVES 6 •

HOT HONEY

1 cup (240 ml) honey

⅓ cup (80 ml) Crystal® Hot Sauce

SPICE BLEND

½ cup (44 g) dried oregano

½ cup (22 g) dried thyme

2 tbsp (17 g) garlic powder

2 tbsp (14 g) onion powder

2 tbsp (14 g) smoked paprika

1 tsp ground black pepper

1 tsp cayenne pepper

1 tsp ground cumin

1 tsp ground coriander

CAULIFLOWER

1 tsp sugar

1 tsp kosher salt

¾ cup (48 g) + ¼ cup (16 g) Spice Blend, divided

4 cups (960 ml) water

1 head cauliflower, cored and broken into florets

4 cups (960 ml) vegetable oil for frying

1 cup (125 g) all-purpose flour

Maldon sea salt flakes or kosher salt

To make the hot honey, pour the honey and hot sauce in a small bowl and stir to combine. Set aside until needed.

To make the spice blend, place all the ingredients in a medium mixing bowl and stir to combine. Store in an airtight container until needed.

To make the cauliflower, place the sugar, salt, ¾ cup (48 g) of the spice blend and water in a large pot over high heat and bring to a boil. After 3 minutes of boiling, remove from the heat and add the cauliflower. Let cool, cover and refrigerate for 36 hours.

In a tabletop fryer or a large, heavy pot over medium-high heat, add the oil. Heat to 350°F (175°C).

In a large bowl, add the flour and remaining ¼ cup (16 g) of the spice blend and stir to combine. Drain the cauliflower and dredge it in the seasoned flour, shaking off any excess. Carefully add the breaded cauliflower pieces to the hot oil and fry until they're golden brown, about 4 minutes. If they don't all fit in the pot at once, work in batches. When each batch is done, remove them to a paper towel–lined plate to drain. Sprinkle with the sea salt flakes or kosher salt and serve immediately with the hot honey dipping sauce.

EXTRA CHEESY GARLIC KNOTS

East Village Pizza, East Village, New York

How do you make a plate of warm, fragrant, fresh-baked garlic knots even better? You pile on a mountain of mozzarella cheese and bake it until it's hot, bubbly and irresistible. At East Village Pizza, Chef Frank Kabatas starts with long-fermented pizza dough, which he ties into knots and bakes until they're golden brown. We cheat a little by starting with prepared dough (though you are encouraged to make your own), but we still pile on the butter, parmesan, fresh garlic and parsley before topping the whole shebang with TWO POUNDS (908 g) of shredded mozzarella. All we can say is get ready for some insane cheese pulls!

MAKES 6 KNOTS •

½ lb (226 g) prepared refrigerated pizza dough

½ cup (114 g) butter

¼ cup (25 g) grated parmesan cheese

1 bunch fresh parsley, leaves only, chopped

1 cup (136 g) chopped fresh garlic

8 cups (2 lbs [908 g]) shredded mozzarella cheese

Remove the pizza dough from the refrigerator and allow it to come to room temperature.

Preheat the oven to 500°F (260°C).

Cut the dough into six equal pieces. Working with one piece at a time, roll them into ropes and tie each rope in a knot. Arrange the knots on a sheet pan and let rise for 30 minutes. Then bake the knots until they are golden brown, about 15 minutes.

While the knots are baking, in a small saucepan over medium heat, melt the butter. When the knots are baked, remove them to a large bowl and drizzle with melted butter. Top with the parmesan cheese, parsley and garlic and toss to coat. Let sit for 3 minutes.

Arrange the knots in an oven-safe dish, top with the mozzarella and bake until the cheese is completely melted, about 15 minutes.

CHEF'S NOTE: Add more or less parsley, as you like.

KALE PESTO–STUFFED BURRATA

The Bedford, Williamsburg, Brooklyn

This dish is an absolute showstopper. In its common form, burrata is a ball of soft cheese that oozes milky cream when sliced open. This amazing version is double-stuffed with creamy curds and kale pesto, which adds vivid color and flavor to the party. Chef Sean Rawlinson came up with the clever idea to take sauces that he normally uses on top of burrata and instead place them inside the cheese. The results speak for themselves. We recommend serving these with warm grilled pita, crackers or bread along with a side salad and a drizzle of balsamic.

MAKES 3 BURRATA BALLS •

KALE PESTO

2 cups (134 g) packed kale leaves, stems discarded and leaves torn into pieces

1 cup (24 g) packed fresh basil leaves

1 tsp sea salt

¼ cup (60 ml) extra-virgin olive oil

4 cloves garlic, chopped

¼ cup (29 g) toasted walnuts

½ cup (50 g) grated parmesan cheese

BURRATA

5 tbsp (70 g) kosher salt, divided

1½ lbs (680 g) mozzarella curd cheese, divided (see Chef's Note, next page)

4 cups (960 ml) heavy cream

To make the kale pesto, place the kale, basil and salt in a blender or food processor. Pulse until they're finely chopped, making sure to scrape down the sides a few times. With the machine running, add the olive oil in a slow, steady stream. Stop and scrape down the sides again. Add the garlic and walnuts and pulse a few times. Add the parmesan and pulse to combine. Set aside until needed.

To make the burrata, place a large pot over medium heat. Add 2 quarts (1.9 L) of water and 2 tablespoons (28 g) of the kosher salt and bring to a boil. Submerge one-third (½ lb [226 g]) of the cheese curds in the boiling water until it's heated through, about 3 minutes. Wearing heat-resistant gloves, lift the cheese out of the water and hold it above the pot. Knead the cheese until the curds come together and you can start to stretch and fold the cheese onto itself. As the cheese cools, dunk it in the hot water to warm it. After about 10 minutes of kneading, the cheese should be smooth and glossy. Shred and tear it into small pieces resembling cottage cheese and place in a large bowl. Add the cream and 1 tablespoon (14 g) of the kosher salt, stir to combine and set aside.

(continued)

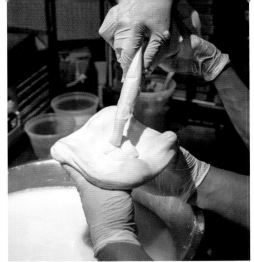

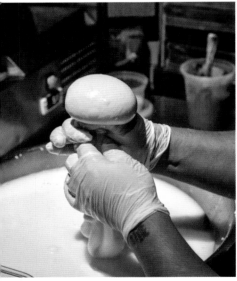

KALE PESTO–STUFFED BURRATA (CONT.)

Discard the hot water and rinse the pot. To make the burrata balls, add 2 quarts (1.9 L) of water and the remaining 2 tablespoons (28 g) of kosher salt and bring to a boil. Divide the remaining cheese curds into three even portions and repeat the warming, stretching and folding process with each. When each piece turns smooth, glossy and elastic, stretch it into a 6-inch (15-cm) disc. Put the discs back in the hot water.

Working with one disc at a time, push the cheese into a small bowl to form an open pocket. Fill each with one-third of the creamy curd mixture and 2 tablespoons (30 ml) of the kale pesto. Fold the cheese and pinch the edges together to form a sealed pouch. Dip the edges in hot water to help seal it shut. Transfer to a bowl of cold water to firm, about 15 minutes. Repeat the filling and sealing process with the remaining two pieces of cheese.

CHEF'S NOTE: While not exactly common, mozzarella cheese curd can be found at many Italian groceries as well as online retailers.

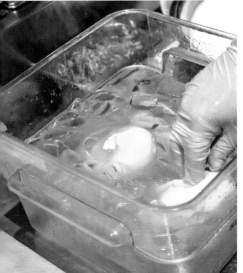

CHICKEN TINGA NACHOS

Roebling Sporting Club, Williamsburg, Brooklyn

Everybody loves nachos, including Chef Sean Rawlinson. But for his sports bar–themed menu, he wanted to reinvent the pub grub staple. "Nachos are a hit at sports bars," he says. "But chicken tinga is much more interesting than a plain, boring pulled chicken. The tinga brings a new level." After one bite, we promise that this huge pile of crunchy, spicy goodness will be your new go-to nacho recipe for game day. The adobo-spiced chicken tinga adds an earthy and exotic Mexican twist, while the spicy cheese sauce ties it all together. Invite some hungry guests, because this recipe is built for a crowd.

MAKES 4 SERVINGS

BLACK BEANS

¼ cup (60 ml) canola oil

1 small white onion, chopped

Kosher salt

Black pepper

1 (15.5-oz [439-g]) can black beans, drained

SALSA FRESCA

2 beefsteak tomatoes, diced

½ medium white onion, diced

1 jalapeño pepper, seeded and diced

1 bunch fresh cilantro, chopped

¼ cup (60 ml) lime juice

Kosher salt

Black pepper

CHEESE SAUCE

2 cups (480 ml) heavy cream

3 lbs (1.4 kg) American cheese, roughly chopped

½ cup (120 g) pickled jalapeño peppers, chopped

Kosher salt

Black pepper

To make the black beans, place a large saucepan over medium heat. Add the oil followed by the onion and pinches of salt and pepper. Cook, stirring occasionally, until the onion turns translucent, about 5 minutes. Add the black beans and cook for 15 minutes to infuse the flavor. Remove from the heat, allow to cool, cover and refrigerate until needed.

To make the salsa fresca, add the tomatoes, onion, jalapeño and cilantro to a large bowl and stir to combine. Add the lime juice and season to taste with salt and pepper. Cover and refrigerate until needed.

To make the cheese sauce, place a large saucepan over medium heat and add the cream. When the cream is hot, add the cheese one handful at a time, waiting until each batch is melted before adding more. When all the cheese has been added and melted, add the jalapeños. Season to taste with salt and pepper.

(continued)

CHICKEN TINGA

5 lbs (2.3 kg) boneless, skinless chicken breasts

1 medium white onion, quartered

2 cloves garlic

2 tbsp (28 g) kosher salt, divided

2 cups (480 ml) chicken stock

1 (7-oz [198-g]) can chipotle peppers in adobo sauce

¼ cup (60 ml) canola oil

½ medium white onion, chopped

4 tomatoes, chopped

1 tbsp (7 g) smoked paprika

1 tbsp (8 g) ground cumin

1 tbsp (6 g) black pepper

ASSEMBLY

1 (18-ounce [510-g]) bag tortilla chips

1 cup (226 g) Chicken Tinga, warmed

1 cup (172 g) Black Beans, warmed

1 cup (240 ml) Cheese Sauce, warmed

6 tbsp (108 g) Salsa Fresca

6 tbsp (90 ml) sour cream

6 tbsp (38 g) sliced jalapeño peppers

1½ tbsp (11 g) sliced radishes

1½ tbsp (2 g) chopped fresh cilantro

CHICKEN TINGA NACHOS (CONT.)

To make the chicken tinga, place a large pot over medium heat and add the chicken breasts, the quartered onion, garlic, 1 tablespoon (14 g) of salt and the chicken stock. Bring to a simmer and cook for 30 minutes. Remove the cooked chicken from the stock. When it's cool enough to handle, use two forks to shred the meat and set aside. Transfer the contents of the pot (minus the chicken) to a blender or food processor, add the chipotle peppers in adobo sauce and process until smooth. Set aside.

Return the pot to medium heat and add the canola oil followed by the chopped onion. Cook, stirring occasionally, until the onion turns translucent, about 5 minutes. Add the tomatoes, shredded chicken, paprika, cumin, remaining tablespoon (14 g) of salt, pepper and the puréed chicken stock mixture and bring to a simmer. Cook for 20 minutes. Taste and adjust the seasoning, adding additional salt and pepper if desired.

To assemble the chicken tinga nachos, place the tortilla chips on a plate. Top with the chicken tinga, black beans, cheese sauce, salsa fresca, sour cream, jalapeños, radishes and cilantro.

FRIES WITH THE WORKS

Blue Ribbon Fried Chicken, East Village, New York

Every other bar in New York serves some type of cheesy fries. We know, because we've tried almost all of them. What we love about this version, served at one of our favorite fried chicken haunts, is the addition of sour cream to the fries before—not after—they bake. It elevates the gooey, melty, stretchy texture of the cheddar cheese. And what more needs to be said about crispy bacon other than it's literally the best garnish for every type of food. When it comes to the spicy seasoning mix, go crazy. We love it HOT, so we double the amount of cayenne pepper.

MAKES 2 SERVINGS ·

SPICY SEASONING MIX

2 tsp (5 g) smoked paprika

1½ tsp (9 g) salt

½ tsp garlic powder

½ tsp onion powder

½ tsp dried ground parsley

½ tsp dried ground basil

¼ tsp cayenne pepper

FRIES

4 large russet potatoes

Nonstick cooking spray

4 slices bacon

4 cups (960 ml) vegetable oil

2 tbsp (13 g) Spicy Seasoning Mix

6 tbsp (90 ml) sour cream

2 cups (226 g) shredded cheddar cheese

To make the spicy seasoning mix, combine all the ingredients in a small container and mix well. Set aside until needed.

To make the fries, peel and rinse the potatoes. With a sharp knife and a steady hand, cut them into ¼-inch (6-mm)-thick sticks. Put them in a large bowl and add enough cold water to cover. Refrigerate until needed.

Place a medium skillet over medium heat. Lightly spray the pan with nonstick cooking spray. Add the bacon and cook, turning once halfway through, until it's fully cooked and crispy, about 4 minutes per side. Transfer to a paper towel–lined plate to drain. When the bacon is cool enough to handle, dice it and set aside until needed.

In a tabletop fryer or a large, heavy pot over medium-high heat, heat the oil to 350°F (175°C). Drain and towel dry the potatoes and carefully add them to the hot oil. Cook until they're golden brown and crisp, about 7 minutes. Transfer to a paper towel–lined plate to drain.

Preheat the oven to 400°F (205°C).

Season the fries with the seasoning mix and arrange in a pile on a sheet pan. Top with the sour cream and cheddar cheese and bake until the cheese has melted, about 4 minutes. Top with the bacon and continue cooking until the bacon is hot and crisp, about 3 minutes.

BRONSON FRIES

Fedoroff's Roast Pork, Williamsburg, Brooklyn; Financial District, New York

These fries are famous! They were created by New York celebrity Action Bronson while he was filming an episode of his TV food show at Fedoroff's. The recipe essentially is a Philly cheesesteak that swaps the hoagie bun for French fries—and if that doesn't sound f—in' delicious, we don't know what does! Piled on top of a mountain of cheesesteak fries is a heaping handful of sliced hot cherry peppers, which absolutely make the dish. This might be the best plate of cheese fries in the whole world—and we stand by that statement.

MAKES 1 SERVING . . . .

1 large russet potato

4 cups (960 ml) + 1 tbsp (15 ml) canola oil, divided

1 small yellow onion, diced

½ lb (226 g) top round beef, preferably USDA Prime, very thinly sliced

5 slices American cheese

½ cup (60 g) sliced hot cherry peppers (such as B&G® brand)

Peel and rinse the potato. With a sharp knife and a steady hand, cut it into ¼-inch (6-mm)-thick sticks. Put them in a medium bowl and add enough cold water to cover. Refrigerate until needed.

In a tabletop fryer or a large, heavy pot over medium-high heat, preheat 4 cups (960 ml) of the oil to 350°F (175°C).

Drain and towel dry the potatoes and carefully add them to the hot oil. Cook until they're golden brown and crisp, about 7 minutes. Transfer to a paper towel–lined plate to drain.

In a large skillet over medium heat, add the remaining tablespoon (15 ml) of oil, the onion and the steak. Cook, stirring occasionally, until the onion is soft and the steak is well done, about 5 minutes. Carefully pour off any accumulated fat. Arrange the meat and onion in a pile in the skillet and top with the sliced American cheese. While you're waiting for the cheese to melt, transfer the fries to a plate. When the cheese is fully melted, turn off the heat and place the meat and cheese pile on top of the fries. Top with sliced cherry peppers and enjoy.

SLOW-COOKED BOURBON-GLAZED BACON

Del Frisco's Double Eagle Steakhouse, Midtown, New York

We love taking out-of-town friends to Del Frisco's in Midtown because it offers such a quintessential NYC experience. And when we're there, we have to get the extra-thick, extra-juicy bourbon-glazed bacon. At the restaurant, Chef Ariel Fox starts with sous vide bacon, but he adapted this recipe for home cooks. "The sous vide bacon is definitely a favorite among guests at the Double Eagle because it's so rich and over-the-top," he says. "We wanted to share a version of this dish that anyone at home can make in a regular oven." Thanks, chef!

MAKES 8 SERVINGS •

BOURBON GLAZE

1 cup (240 ml) white vinegar

¾ cup (180 ml) molasses

¾ cup (180 ml) orange juice concentrate

¼ cup (60 ml) bourbon

⅛ cup (30 ml) honey

Juice of 1 lime

¾ cup (150 g) granulated sugar

⅛ tsp kosher salt

⅛ tsp black pepper

BACON

2 lbs (907 g) slab bacon

1 tbsp (6 g) coarsely ground black pepper

1 cup (240 ml) Bourbon Glaze, divided

1 Fresno chili, thinly sliced

To make the bourbon glaze, place a medium saucepan over medium-high heat. Add the white vinegar, molasses, orange juice concentrate, bourbon, honey, lime juice, sugar, salt and pepper and bring to a boil. Lower the heat to medium and simmer until the liquid has reduced to 1 cup (240 ml), about 20 to 25 minutes. Set aside to cool.

Preheat the oven to 350°F (175°C). Line a baking sheet with foil or parchment paper.

Arrange the bacon slab fat side up on the lined baking sheet. With a sharp knife, make a crosshatch of five or six ½-inch (13-mm)-deep diagonal cuts into the fat, making sure not to go all the way into the meat. Season the top with pepper, coat with ½ cup (120 ml) of the bourbon glaze, cover with foil and cook for 1 hour.

Flip the bacon, coat with ½ cup (120 ml) of the bourbon glaze, lower the heat to 325°F (165°C) and continue cooking for 1 hour.

Slice the bacon slab lengthwise into 8 pieces, garnish with the thinly sliced Fresno chili and serve warm.

FRIED PICKLES

Diller, Lower East Side, New York

Diller is a really cool spot on the Lower East Side that does amazing things with pickles, elevating the typical supporting star to the main attraction. It's no surprise that the snack shop is owned by The Pickle Guys, the popular pickle emporium located directly next door. For this recipe, they prefer to use full sour pickles, which burst through all the layers. What makes this fried pickle stand out is the crunchy, one-of-a-kind coating. We suggest serving these with your favorite dipping sauce like a garlic or sriracha aioli.

MAKES 4 SERVINGS

1 tbsp (7 g) flaxseed meal

1 cup (240 ml) water, divided

4 tsp (13 g) rice flour

2 tsp (5 g) tapioca flour

½ tsp baking powder

½ cup (44 g) fine cornmeal

4 cups (412 g) gluten-free rice panko

4 cups (620 g) sour pickles, cut into to ¼-inch (6-mm) slices

1 quart (960 ml) canola oil

In a small bowl, add the flaxseed meal and ¼ cup (60 ml) of water and whisk to blend.

In a medium bowl, add the rice flour, tapioca flour, baking powder, cornmeal, flaxseed mixture and the remaining ¾ cup (180 ml) of water and whisk well to blend. The batter should be slightly thicker than pancake batter.

Pat dry the pickle slices. Add the pickles to the batter and stir to coat. Toss the battered pickles in the rice panko to coat and set aside while the oil heats up (but not more than 25 minutes).

In a tabletop fryer or a large, heavy pot over medium-high heat, add the oil. Heat to 365°F (185°C).

Carefully add the pickle slices one at a time to the hot oil and fry until they're golden brown, about 2 minutes. When each pickle slice is done, remove it to a paper towel–lined plate to drain. Serve with your favorite dipping sauce.

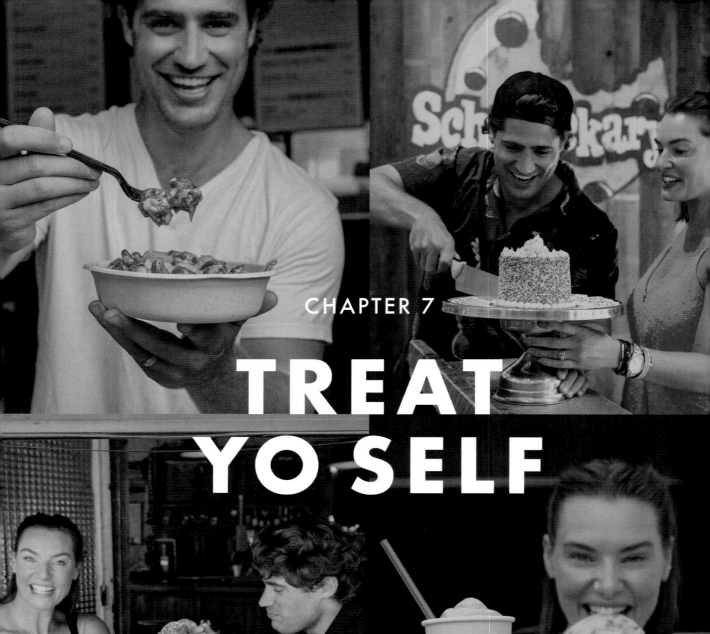

CHAPTER 7

TREAT YO SELF

ALL THINGS SWEET

We're going to be completely honest here: We aren't the biggest dessert lovers in the world. We like what we like, and that's okay. With that being said, the sweets included here have surpassed our very picky taste tests, so we think you'll love them just as much as we do.

We've enlisted some of our favorite bakeries to bring you unique and delectable recipes for that perfect after-dinner treat. Or maybe you want to eat dessert for breakfast—we don't judge. Just know before flipping these pages that you will not find recipes for a boring oatmeal raisin cookie or the kind of cupcakes your mom baked for your teenage birthday parties. Nope, not here.

First stop, the Lower East Side, for the sweetest, stickiest twist on chicken and waffles you have EVER experienced (page 132). But maybe you want to go the ice cream route, with a crunchy, salty twist (page 142). Or travel to Williamsburg, Brooklyn, to indulge in a breakfast-themed gem: French Toast Fritters (page 138). There also is a crazy stacked cookie cake (page 135) and a booze-filled treat that will leave you wondering how on earth you managed to exist all this time without it (page 141).

Have you mastered the art of baking? We think it's time to find out. So dust off those measuring spoons and cups and let the baking challenge begin!

PB&J CHICKEN 'N WAFFLES

375° Chicken 'N Fries, Lower East Side, New York

When we asked chef-owner Stephane Lemagnen how he came up with the idea for this instant smash, he responded, "The real question is, why has nobody done this before?" Everybody's favorite childhood sandwich, the PB&J, is the obvious inspiration for the dish, but it is elevated to new heights thanks to the fried chicken and waffle components and top-notch ingredients and technique. "We like to take a playful approach to food, but we don't cut corners," Lemagnen promises. "We make everything from scratch with real ingredients and we cook everything fresh to order." Most fried chicken recipes are on the savory side, so we appreciate that this one is a little sweet, sticky and gooey.

MAKES 6 SERVINGS •

POPCORN CHICKEN

1 cup (240 ml) buttermilk

½ cup (120 ml) Frank's RedHot cayenne pepper sauce

1 tbsp (18 g) salt

2 lbs (907 g) boneless, skinless chicken breasts, cubed

4 cups (960 ml) canola oil

GRAPE JELLY "JAM"

1 (32-oz [907-g]) jar grape jelly (4 cups [960 ml])

1 (12-oz [340-g]) bottle Heinz® chili sauce (1½ cups [360 ml])

1 (12-oz [340-g]) bottle Heinz ketchup (1½ cups [360 ml])

PEANUT SAUCE

½ cup (129 g) peanut butter

Hot water

To marinate the popcorn chicken, in a medium bowl, add the buttermilk, Frank's RedHot sauce and salt and whisk to combine. Add the cubed chicken, cover and refrigerate for at least 4 hours, but preferably overnight.

To make the grape jelly "jam," combine the grape jelly, chili sauce and ketchup in a saucepan over medium-high heat. Cook until everything is blended and warm, about 5 minutes. Set aside until needed.

To make the peanut sauce, combine the peanut butter with a tablespoon or two (15 to 30 ml) of hot water and stir until the sauce is smooth and creamy. Set aside until needed.

(continued)

CHEESE AND SCALLION WAFFLES

4 cups (500 g) all-purpose flour

1 tsp baking soda

2 tsp (9 g) baking powder

2 tsp (12 g) salt

2 tbsp (30 g) sugar

6 eggs

4 cups (960 ml) buttermilk

6 tbsp (84 g) butter, melted

¾ cup (84 g) shredded Monterey jack cheese

¾ cup (85 g) shredded sharp cheddar cheese

6 scallions, thinly sliced

Nonstick cooking spray

SEASONED FLOUR

2 cups (250 g) all-purpose flour

1 tbsp (14 g) baking powder

2 tsp (12 g) salt

2 tsp (5 g) sweet paprika

1 tbsp (5 g) cayenne pepper

1 tsp celery salt

1 tbsp (6 g) black pepper

1 tbsp (7 g) onion powder

1 tbsp (8 g) garlic powder

PB&J CHICKEN 'N WAFFLES (CONT.)

To make the waffles, add the flour, baking soda, baking powder, salt and sugar to a large bowl and whisk to combine. In a separate large bowl, add the eggs, buttermilk and melted butter and whisk to blend. Add the wet ingredients to the dry ingredients and mix until they're just combined and no pockets of dry flour remain. Fold in the Monterey jack and cheddar cheeses and the scallions.

Preheat a waffle iron. If necessary, spray the waffle iron with nonstick cooking spray. Add 1 cup (240 ml) of batter per waffle and cook until it's golden brown, following the manufacturer's instructions for your waffle iron. Repeat until all the waffles are cooked. Keep the waffles warm until you're ready to serve.

To cook the chicken, in a large bowl, add all of the ingredients for the seasoned flour mixture and whisk to combine. Drain the chicken, discard the marinade and add the chicken to the bowl with the seasoned flour. Toss well to coat. Place the coated chicken in a strainer and lightly toss to shake off any excess flour.

In a tabletop fryer or a large, heavy pot over medium-high heat, add the oil and heat to 350°F (175°C). Carefully add the chicken to the hot oil and fry until it's golden brown, about 4 minutes, or until an instant-read thermometer registers at least 165°F (75°C). Transfer to a paper towel–lined plate to drain. Add the warm chicken to a large bowl, add the grape jelly "jam" and toss to coat.

To serve, top each waffle with some popcorn chicken and drizzle with peanut sauce.

FUNFETTI COOKIE CAKES

Schmackary's, Hell's Kitchen and Cooper Square, New York

Zachary "Schmackary" Schmahl doesn't run just any ordinary cookie shop. He set out to elevate the genre by upgrading from run-of-the-mill chocolate chip and oatmeal raisin cookies to truly unique gourmet treats. Now he offers more than 75 flavors. The fanciful "cakes" in this recipe are made by stacking layer upon layer of sugar-crusted cookies with frosting and then covering the whole thing in rainbow nonpareils and more frosting. We think this is one of the most inventive (and gorgeous) uses of cookies we've ever seen!

MAKES 4 COOKIE CAKES •

Nonstick cooking spray

COOKIES
2 cups (250 g) all-purpose flour

½ tsp baking powder

½ tsp kosher salt

1 cup (2 sticks, 227 g) unsalted butter, softened

1½ cups (300 g) sugar, divided

1 tbsp (14 g) light brown sugar

1½ tsp (8 ml) vanilla extract

1 egg

½ cup (80 g) sprinkles

Preheat the oven to 375°F (190°C). Line two large sheet pans with parchment paper or spray with nonstick cooking spray. Set aside.

In a medium bowl, add the flour, baking powder and salt and stir to combine. Set aside.

In the bowl of a stand mixer fitted with the paddle attachment, add the butter, 1 cup (200 g) of the sugar and the brown sugar, and mix on medium until the mixture is light and fluffy, making sure to scrape down the sides of the bowl occasionally. Add the vanilla and egg and beat until they're blended. Add the dry ingredients and beat until just combined, making sure not to overmix. Add the sprinkles and gently fold to incorporate.

Place the remaining ½ cup (100 g) of sugar in a shallow bowl. Portion the cookie dough into 20 (approximately 3-ounce [85-g]) balls and roll them in the sugar. Arrange the cookies on the prepared sheet pans. Grease the bottom of a heavy glass cup, dip it in sugar and flatten the cookies to a thickness of ¾ inch (19 mm). Redip the glass in sugar as needed until you have flattened all the cookies.

Bake the cookies for about 15 minutes, until they're golden brown around the edges, rotating the pans halfway after the first 10 minutes. Remove the pans from the oven and let the cookies sit on the sheet pans for 3 minutes before transferring them to a wire rack to cool.

(continued)

There's only one cure for a Schmack Attack

FROSTING

½ cup (1 stick, 114 g) unsalted butter, softened

4 cups (480 g) confectioners' sugar

8 oz (226 g) cream cheese

2 tsp (10 ml) vanilla extract

1 (1-lb [454-g]) bag rainbow nonpareils

FUNFETTI COOKIE CAKES (CONT.)

To make the frosting, place the butter and confectioners' sugar in the bowl of a stand mixer fitted with the whisk attachment and blend on medium until they're smooth. Add the cream cheese and vanilla and continue beating until the frosting is well-whipped and smooth, making sure to scrape down the sides of the bowl occasionally. If the frosting is too runny to spread, refrigerate for 15 to 30 minutes until it's firm.

To assemble each cake, start by making a cookie sandwich by connecting two cookies with frosting, arranging them bottom side out. Stack on three more cookies, using frosting to join them, so you have a five-cookie stack. Repeat with the remaining cookies until you have four separate five-cookie stacks. Use your hands to straighten and lightly compress each stack. Place in the freezer to chill for 20 minutes.

Working with one stack at a time, place a dollop of frosting on a cake stand or plate and position a cookie tower in the center, making sure it is perpendicular. Using a paring knife, trim off any protruding cookie edges to smooth the exterior as much as possible. Using an offset spatula, apply frosting to fill in the gaps between each cookie. Continue applying this "crumb coat" until all sides are covered and smooth. Return to the freezer for 20 minutes. Apply another thin, smooth layer of frosting to the entire cake and return to the freezer for 10 minutes. Repeat this process with the remaining cookie towers.

Place the rainbow nonpareils in a large bowl. Holding steady one cookie tower at a time and working from the bottom to the top, apply nonpareils to the exterior by lightly pressing them on with your free hand. Continue applying until all sides and tops are evenly coated. Repeat this process with the remaining cookie towers.

Transfer the remaining frosting to a pastry bag fitted with a large star tip. Pipe baby rosettes around the base of each cake and the perimeter of each cake top. Pipe one large rosette onto the middle of each tower top. Store the cookie cakes at room temperature.

FRENCH TOAST FRITTERS
Roebling Sporting Club, Williamsburg, Brooklyn

Chef Sean Rawlinson makes some of our all-time favorite pub grub (see the Chicken Tinga Nachos on page 119!) and these golden-brown French Toast Fritters are no exception. This is sweet-and-sticky finger food all the way, which makes it perfect for a sports bar. Crunchy on the outside, warm and gooey on the inside, this breakfast-themed dessert will leave you scrambling for more.

MAKES 4 SERVINGS •

NUTELLA CURRANT JAM

½ quart (224 g) ripe red currants, stemmed

1 cup (200 g) sugar

⅛ cup (30 ml) water

½ cup (148 g) Nutella®

FRENCH TOAST FRITTERS

8 slices brioche bread

2 eggs

¼ cup (60 ml) milk

1 tbsp (15 g) sugar

1 tsp cinnamon

1 tbsp (15 ml) vanilla extract

3 tbsp (42 g) butter

Powdered sugar

To make the Nutella currant jam, place a nonreactive saucepan over medium-low heat. Add the currants and crush them with a wooden spoon. Add the sugar and water and cook, stirring occasionally, until the sugar is completely dissolved. Increase the heat to medium and bring to a boil. Cook until the jam thickens and sets, about 10 minutes. Remove from the heat and skim off any foam that has formed on the surface. When the jam is cool, stir in the Nutella. Transfer the mixture to a pastry bag and set aside until needed.

To make the French toast fritters, cut each slice of bread into four pieces. Wet your hands with a little warm water and roll each piece into a tight ball. With your thumb, make an indentation about halfway into each ball. Pipe some Nutella currant jam into each ball and pinch the bread closed to seal it back up.

In a medium bowl, add the eggs, milk, sugar, cinnamon and vanilla and whisk to combine. Add the stuffed bread balls and toss to coat.

Place a large skillet over medium heat and add the butter. When the foaming subsides, add the bread balls and cook, turning frequently, until they're golden brown, about 3 minutes. Dust with powdered sugar and serve warm.

CHEF'S NOTE: If you don't have a piping bag, a handy trick is to use a plastic zip-top bag instead. Place the mixture into the bag, squeeze it into one corner and cut the tip off. Pipe away!

WOOKIES

Echo Bravo, Bushwick, Brooklyn

What do you get when you marry whiskey and cookies? Wookies, of course! These playful (albeit adult-only) treats are the brainchild of Katherine Buenaflor Dillon, chef-owner of Echo Bravo in the Bushwick neighborhood of Brooklyn. Whiskey-soaked cranberries are spiked with fiery habanero peppers and paired with sweet white chocolate. "Playing with spirits and desserts brings extra joy that our customers certainly appreciate!" says the chef, adding that home cooks should definitely sip some whiskey while baking.

MAKES 36 COOKIES •

1 cup (121 g) dried cranberries

6 tbsp (90 ml) whiskey

1 tsp habanero chili powder

Nonstick cooking spray or butter

2 cups (250 g) all-purpose flour

1 tsp baking powder

½ tsp baking soda

½ tsp kosher salt

1 cup (227 g) butter, slightly softened

¼ cup (52 g) vegetable shortening

1 cup (220 g) brown sugar

¼ cup (50 g) sugar

1 egg

3 tbsp (45 ml) light corn syrup

3 cups (270 g) old-fashioned rolled oats

2 cups (340 g) white chocolate chunks

In a small saucepan over medium-high heat, add the cranberries, whiskey and habanero chili powder and bring to a boil. Remove from the heat, cover and set aside for at least 20 minutes to allow the cranberries to absorb most of the liquid. Drain the cranberries and set aside.

Preheat the oven to 350°F (175°C). Grease 2 large sheet pans with nonstick cooking spray.

In a large bowl, add the flour, baking powder, baking soda and salt and stir to combine. Set aside.

In the bowl of a stand mixer fitted with the paddle attachment, add the butter, shortening, brown sugar and sugar and mix on medium until they're creamy, about 2 minutes. Add the egg and corn syrup and beat until fluffy, about 2 minutes. Add the flour mixture and stir until everything is well blended, about 2 minutes. Add the oats, white chocolate and cranberries and mix to combine. Refrigerate the cookie dough for 10 minutes.

Form the cookie dough into tablespoon-sized (15-g) balls and arrange them on the greased sheet pans, making sure to space them 3 inches (7 cm) apart (baking in batches if needed). Lightly flatten each ball with the back of a spoon and bake until the edges are golden brown, about 12 minutes. Transfer the wookies to a rack to cool before serving. Store in an airtight container.

MILK 'N CHIPS

375° Chicken 'N Fries, Lower East Side, New York

Chef-owner Stephane Lemagnen's goal in conceiving this recipe was straightforward but ambitious: "To create a dessert that combines the most devour-able, crave-able sensations—sweet, salty, creamy, crunchy—all in one cup," he explains. "Bingo!" The salty crunch from the homemade potato chips combined with the cool and creamy ice cream is a match made in dessert heaven. What ties it all together is the warm and wonderful flavor of maple syrup. You'll never reach for plain old ice cream again! You'll need an ice cream maker, but we promise the results are worth the investment.

MAKES 4 SERVINGS •

ICE CREAM

1½ cups (360 ml) heavy cream

6 large egg yolks

1½ cups (360 ml) whole milk

2 tbsp (30 g) sugar

¾ cup (180 ml) pure maple syrup

¼ tsp sea salt

½ tsp vanilla extract

MAPLE-BUTTER POTATO CHIPS

2 russet potatoes, peeled and thinly sliced on a mandoline

4 cups (960 ml) canola oil

1 cup (240 ml) pure maple syrup, plus more for serving

4 tbsp (57 g) butter

Pinch of salt

To start the ice cream, place the cream in a large bowl and set aside.

Place the egg yolks in a medium bowl, beat with a whisk to combine and set aside.

In a medium saucepan over medium heat, add the milk and sugar and heat until they're warm, stirring to dissolve the sugar. Slowly pour the warm milk and sugar mixture into the beaten egg yolks while whisking constantly. Pour this mixture back into the saucepan over medium-low heat. Stir the mixture constantly with a spatula until it coats the back of a spoon and an instant-read thermometer registers 180°F (85°C). Be careful not to let it come to a boil or the custard will curdle.

Add the custard to the bowl with the cream and stir to combine. Strain the mixture through a fine-mesh sieve into a large bowl. Add the maple syrup, sea salt and vanilla and stir to combine. Cover and refrigerate until it's fully chilled, at least 2 hours. Freeze the ice cream according to your ice cream maker's instructions.

To make the maple-butter potato chips, place the potato slices in a bowl of cold water to rinse off any excess starch. Drain the potato slices and arrange them on paper towels to dry.

In a tabletop fryer or a large, heavy pot over medium-high heat, add the oil. Heat to 350°F (175°C). Carefully add the potatoes and fry until they're golden brown, about 4 minutes. If they don't all fit in the pot at once, work in batches. When each batch is done, remove it to a paper towel–lined plate to drain.

In a small saucepan over medium-high heat, add the maple syrup, butter and salt and bring to a boil. Remove from the heat to cool.

Place the potato chips in a large bowl, top with the cooled maple syrup mixture and toss to coat.

To serve, crush a generous amount of potato chips and place them in the bottoms of four bowls. Top each with a scoop of ice cream, sprinkle more crushed potato chips on top and drizzle with a little maple syrup.

THANK-YOUS

First and foremost, we want to thank *all* of the chefs and business owners who participated in this project. We could not have done it without all of your efforts, talent and participation. You have shared a little piece of your heart in the form of a recipe that took your blood, sweat and tears to create, and we are so grateful for that. A good portion of this book was written during the COVID-19 quarantine, but that didn't stop the outpouring of support from everyone involved. It shows how much the hospitality industry steps up and supports one another in times of crisis, and for that we cannot thank you all enough.

Also, we'd like to thank our parents, Denise Remmey and Denise and Michael McMahon, who have always been the number-one fans of our food-filled adventures. When we quit our "normal" jobs to pursue our shared passions for food and travel, each offered words of encouragement and support, and we've never looked back. Additionally, to our late fathers, William Remmey and Jonathan West, you both had a huge impact on our lives when it came to food, and we know you both would absolutely love this book.

Next, we'd like to thank all of our fans and followers at @DEVOURPOWER for your love, likes, comments, direct messages, emails and kind words. You motivate us to do more, work harder and keep on growing!

We want to give a huge thank-you to Douglas Trattner, our recipe editor, who was a rock star during this whole process. Not many people can handle recipes from 50 different chefs and restaurant owners flying at them at all hours of the day, but he did so without skipping a beat. We are so grateful to have worked with this veteran cookbook author for our first book.

And last, but by no means least, to everyone at Page Street Publishing for giving us this opportunity and paving the way for success at every step. We wouldn't even know where to begin without such a talented team in our corner.

ABOUT THE AUTHORS

Greg Remmey and Rebecca West-Remmey are the founders and faces of @DEVOURPOWER, a world-renowned food and travel blog with more than 2 million followers. Living in Brooklyn, New York, the influencer couple launched their business in 2012 and now run the social media marketing firm Devour Media LLC. Together they have hosted a number of prominent events, including some for the New York City Wine & Food Festival, where they teamed up with Adam Richman of the Travel Channel and the cast of Food Network's *Chopped*. Greg and Rebecca have appeared on the Food Network's original digital series *Munch Rush* and have made guest appearances on *Experimental Eats*. They have been featured in *Cosmopolitan, Adweek,* Refinery29, MR PORTER and MIC, among other publications.

INDEX

Symbols

375° Chicken 'N Fries, 132, 142

A

Abdoo, Matt, 55, 81
Action Bronson, 125
aioli
  Black Pepper Aioli, 27
  Paprika Aioli, 38
American cheese
  Bacon Onion Jam "Magic" Smash
    Burger, 55
  Bronson Fries, 125
  Bulgogi Cheesesteak Tacos, 100
  Chicken Tinga Nachos, 119
  Loaded Doritos® Grilled Cheese, 20
  Philly Cheesesteak, 23
  Scrapple & Egg Burger, 52
  Shrimp Big Mac 'n' Cheese Burger,
    41–43
Anthony and Son Panini Shoppe, 19
appetizers
  Bronson Fries, 125
  Chicken Tinga Nachos, 119–121
  Dynamite Mac & Cheese Balls, 111
  Extra Cheesy Garlic Knots, 115
  Fried Pickles, 129
  Fries with the Works, 122
  Kale Pesto–Stuffed Burrata, 116–118
  Kentucky Fried Cauliflower with Hot
    Honey, 112
  Slow-Cooked Bourbon-Glazed Bacon,
    126
arugula: Beer Cheese Burger, 47
At the Wallace, 56
avocados
  Beer Cheese Burger, 47
  The Butch Hero, 19
  Loaded Carne Asada Quesadillas,
    97–99
  Loaded Doritos® Grilled Cheese, 20
  Steak Burrito with Kettle Queso, 94

B

bacon
  Bacon Onion Jam, 55
  Bacon Onion Jam "Magic" Smash
    Burger, 55
  The Butch Hero, 19
  Charred Pork Ribs, 91
  Fries with the Works, 122
  Hoisin Barbecue Sauce, 91
  Loaded Doritos® Grilled Cheese, 20
  Mango Habanero Bacon Wings, 84
  Pancake Burrito, 103

Slow-Cooked Bourbon-Glazed Bacon,
    126
  The Steez Dog, 56
  Wake and Bake Burger, 48
baguettes: Pepperoni Pizza Cheesesteak,
    16
Ballaney, Deepak, 78
The Bedford, 38–40, 116
beef, ground
  Bacon Onion Jam "Magic" Smash
    Burger, 55
  Beer Cheese Burger, 47
  Cheese Sauce, 33
  Chili, 44, 51
  Chili Cheeseburger, 51
  Chopped Cheese Hero, 33
  Scrapple & Egg Burger, 52
  Texas Hotdog, 44
  Wake and Bake Burger, 48
beef patties
  Chili Cheeseburger, 51
  Mac & Cheese Burger and Fries, 38–40
  Shrimp Big Mac 'n' Cheese Burger,
    41–43
beef ribeye steak
  Bulgogi Cheesesteak Tacos, 100
  Pepperoni Pizza Cheesesteak, 16
beef short ribs
  Bacon Onion Jam "Magic" Smash
    Burger, 55
  Beer Cheese Burger, 47
  Steak Burrito with Kettle Queso, 94
beef skirt steak: Loaded Carne Asada
    Quesadillas, 97–99
beef top round
  Bronson Fries, 125
  Pepperoni Pizza Cheesesteak, 16
  Philly Cheesesteak, 23
beer
  Beer Cheese, 47
  Beer Cheese Burger, 47
Bella Gioia, 74
bell peppers
  Bulgogi Cheesesteak Tacos, 100
  Cheese Sauce, 33
  Chili, 44, 51
  Chili Cheeseburger, 51
  Chimichurri Sauce, 63
  Chopped Cheese Hero, 33
  Dominican Pizza, 63–64
  Firecracker Wings, 78–80
  Pepperoni Pizza Cheesesteak, 16
  Texas Hotdog, 44
Bensons, 47
black beans
  Chicken Tinga Nachos, 119–121
  Steak Burrito with Kettle Queso, 96
Blue Ribbon Fried Chicken
  Fries with the Works, 122

The Panino Supremo Sandwich, 24
Brine Chicken, 27–28
Bronson Fries, 125
Buffalo Chicken Pizza, 69
Bulgogi Cheesesteak Tacos, 100
Burger, Inc., 111
burgers
  Bacon Onion Jam "Magic" Smash
    Burger, 55
  Beer Cheese Burger, 47
  Chili Cheeseburger, 51
  Mac & Cheese Burger and Fries, 38–40
  Scrapple & Egg Burger, 52
  Shrimp Big Mac 'n' Cheese Burger,
    41–43
  Wake and Bake Burger, 48
burrata
  Burrata Pizza, 60
  Kale Pesto–Stuffed Burrata, 116–118
  Lobster Burrata Pasta, 74
burritos
  Mac Wrap with Smoked Pastrami, 107
  Pancake Burrito, 103
  Steak Burrito with Kettle Queso, 94–96
The Butch Hero, 19

C

Cachapas y Mas, 29, 44
cake: Funfetti Cookie Cakes, 135–137
Capon, Josh, 55
Carolina reaper chilies
  Chili Sauce, 78
  Firecracker Wings, 78
carrots
  Grilled Coleslaw, 28
  Pulled Chicken Sandwich, 27–28
Cash, Corey, 107
Cash Only BBQ, 107
cauliflower: Kentucky Fried Cauliflower
    with Hot Honey, 112
challah: The Panino Supremo Sandwich,
    24
Charred Pork Ribs, 91
cheddar cheese
  Beer Cheese, 47
  Beer Cheese Burger, 47
  Bulgogi Cheesesteak Tacos, 100
  Cheese and Scallion Waffles, 134
  Cheese Sauce, 33
  Chili Cheeseburger, 51
  Chopped Cheese Hero, 33
  Dynamite Mac & Cheese Balls, 111
  Fries with the Works, 122
  Impossible™ Tacos, 104
  Kettle Queso, 96
  Loaded Doritos® Grilled Cheese, 20
  Mac-and-Cheese Buns, 40
  Mac & Cheese Burger and Fries, 38–40
  Mac Wrap with Smoked Pastrami, 107

Nashville Hot Chicken Pizza, 65
Pancake Burrito, 103
PB&J Chicken 'N Waffles, 132–134
Pepperoni Pizza Mac & Cheese, 73
Shrimp Big Mac 'n' Cheese Burger,
    41–43
Steak Burrito with Kettle Queso, 94–96
The Steez Dog, 56
Wake and Bake Burger, 48
cheesesteak
    Bronson Fries, 125
    Bulgogi Cheesesteak Tacos, 100
    Pepperoni Pizza Cheesesteak, 16
    Philly Cheesesteak, 23
Cheese Wiz: Philly Cheesesteak, 23
Chef Papi Kitchens, 33, 63
cherry peppers
    Bronson Fries, 125
    Philly Cheesesteak, 23
chicken breasts
    Chicken Tinga Nachos, 119–121
    Dominican Pizza, 63–64
    PB&J Chicken 'N Waffles, 132–134
    Pulled Chicken Sandwich, 27–28
chicken cutlets
    Buffalo Chicken Pizza, 69
    The Panino Supremo Sandwich, 24
chicken thighs
    Nashville Hot Chicken Pizza, 65–66
    Pulled Chicken Sandwich, 27–28
chicken wings
    Firecracker Wings, 78–80
    General Tso's Pig Wings, 88
    Grilled BBQ Buffalo Wings with Ala-
        bama White Sauce, 81–83
    Mango Habanero Bacon Wings, 84
    Smoky Manhattan Wings, 87
Chili
    Chili Cheeseburger, 51
    Texas Hotdog, 44
chipotle peppers
    Charred Pork Ribs, 91
    Chicken Tinga Nachos, 119–121
    Hoisin Barbecue Sauce, 91
    Kettle Queso, 96
    Steak Burrito with Kettle Queso, 94–96
    Wake and Bake Burger, 48
Chopped Cheese Hero, 33
cocoa powder
    Chili Sauce, 78
    Firecracker Wings, 78
cod: Sake-Battered Fish & Chips Sando,
    34
coleslaw: Grilled Coleslaw, 28
Conmigo, 94
cookies
    Funfetti Cookie Cakes, 135–137
    Wookies, 141
cranberries: Wookies, 141
cream cheese: Funfetti Cookie Cakes,
    135–137
cucumber
    Chopped Cheese Hero, 33

Dominican Pizza, 63
Papi's Sauce, 33, 63
currants
    French Toast Fritters, 138
    Nutella Currant Jam, 138

D

Daniele, Nico, 74
Del Frisco's Double Eagle Steakhouse,
    126
Demiris, Billy, 94
Diller
    Fried Pickles, 129
    Impossible™ Tacos, 104
Dillon, Katherine Buenaflor, 88, 141
Dominican Pizza, 63–64
Dominican salami: Dominican Pizza,
    63–64
Doritos®: Loaded Doritos® Grilled
    Cheese, 20
Dos Toros Taqueria, 97
Dyckman Dogs, 44

E

East Village Pizza
    Buffalo Chicken Pizza, 69
    Extra Cheesy Garlic Knots, 115
Echo Bravo
    Scrapple & Egg Burger, 52
    Wookies, 141
eggs
    Dynamite Mac & Cheese Balls, 111
    French Toast Fritters, 138
    Funfetti Cookie Cakes, 135–137
    Mac-and-Cheese Buns, 40
    Mac & Cheese Burger and Fries, 40
    Milk 'N Chips, 142
    Pancake Burrito, 103
    The Panino Supremo Sandwich, 24
    PB&J Chicken 'N Waffles, 132–134
    Sake-Battered Fish & Chips Sando, 34
    Scrapple & Egg Burger, 52
    Wake and Bake Burger, 48
    Wookies, 141
Emmy Squared, 65
Extra Cheesy Garlic Knots, 115

F

Fedoroff, Dave, 23, 88
Fedoroff's Roast Pork
    Bronson Fries, 125
    Philly Cheesesteak, 23
Fedoroff, Stella, 23, 88
fior di latte: Burrata Pizza, 60
Firecracker Wings, 78–80
Flip 'N Toss
    Pepperoni Pizza Mac & Cheese, 73
    Shrimp Big Mac 'n' Cheese Burger,
        41–43
Fox, Ariel, 126

French Toast Fritters, 138
Fresno chili peppers: Slow-Cooked Bour-
    bon-Glazed Bacon, 126
fried onions
    Scrapple & Egg Burger, 52
    Texas Hotdog, 44
Fried Pickles, 129
fries
    Bronson Fries, 125
    Fries with the Works, 122
    Mac & Cheese Burger and Fries, 38–40
Funfetti Cookie Cakes, 135–137

G

garlic
    Beer Cheese, 47
    Beer Cheese Burger, 47
    Bulgogi Cheesesteak Tacos, 100
    Burrata Pizza, 60
    Cheese Sauce, 33
    Chicken Tinga Nachos, 119–121
    Chili, 44, 51
    Chili Cheeseburger, 51
    Chili Garlic Sauce, 27
    Chimichurri Sauce, 63
    Chopped Cheese Hero, 33
    Dominican Pizza, 63–64
    Extra Cheesy Garlic Knots, 115
    Firecracker Wings, 78–80
    Garlic Confit, 27
    General Tso's Pig Wings, 88
    Impossible™ Tacos, 104
    Kale Pesto, 116
    Kale Pesto–Stuffed Burrata, 116–118
    Loaded Carne Asada Quesadillas,
        97–99
    Lobster Burrata Pasta, 74
    Marinara, 24
    The Panino Supremo Sandwich, 24
    Pepperoni Pizza Mac & Cheese, 73
    Pulled Chicken Sandwich, 27–28
    Salsa Verde Hot Sauce, 97
    Shrimp Big Mac 'n' Cheese Burger,
        41–43
    Shrimp Sauce, 41
    Shrimp Scampi Pizza, 70
    Smashed Plantain Patacon with Roast
        Pork, 29–30
    Steak Burrito with Kettle Queso, 94–96
    The Steez Dog, 56
    Taco Sauce, 104
    Texas Hotdog, 44
    Tomato Sauce, 60, 63
Garlick, Mike, 104
General Tso's Pig Wings, 88
Glaze Teriyaki, 91
green bell peppers
    Bulgogi Cheesesteak Tacos, 100
    Chili, 44
    Pepperoni Pizza Cheesesteak, 16
    Texas Hotdog, 44

Grilled BBQ Buffalo Wings with Alabama White Sauce, 81–83

H

habanero peppers
    Mango Habanero Bacon Wings, 84
    Mango Habanero Sauce, 84
    Wookies, 141
Harlem Public
    Loaded Doritos® Grilled Cheese, 20
    Wake and Bake Burger, 48
hash browns: Wake and Bake Burger, 48
hoagie buns: Philly Cheesesteak, 23
Holy Ground NYC, 87
honey
    Bourbon Glaze, 126
    Chili Sauce, 78
    Firecracker Wings, 78–80
    Garlic Confit, 27
    Hot Honey, 112
    Kentucky Fried Cauliflower with Hot Honey, 112
    Pulled Chicken Sandwich, 27–28
    Slow-Cooked Bourbon-Glazed Bacon, 126
hot dogs
    The Steez Dog, 56
    Texas Hotdog, 44
Hyland, Matthew, 65

I

Impossible™ Tacos, 104
International Wings Factory, 78

J

jalapeño peppers
    Beer Cheese Burger, 47
    Cheese Sauce, 119
    Chicken Tinga Nachos, 119–121
    Chili Cheeseburger, 51
    Chili, 51
    Dynamite Mac & Cheese Balls, 111
    Loaded Carne Asada Quesadillas, 97–99
    Salsa Fresca, 119
    Salsa Verde Hot Sauce, 97
jam
    Bacon Onion Jam, 55
    Grape Jelly "Jam," 132
    Nutella Currant Jam, 138

K

Kabatas, Frank, 69, 115
kale
    Kale Pesto, 116
    Kale Pesto–Stuffed Burrata, 116–118
Kentucky Fried Cauliflower with Hot Honey, 112

kidney beans
    Chili, 51
    Chili Cheeseburger, 51
Krawiec, Mike, 34
Kremer, Leo, 97
Kremer, Oliver, 97
Kunz, Jimmy, 16

L

Lee, Randy, 111
Lemagnen, Stephane, 132, 142
Loaded Carne Asada Quesadillas, 97–99
Loaded Doritos® Grilled Cheese, 20
Lobster Burrata Pasta, 74
longaniza: Dominican Pizza, 64
LoNigro, Joe, 27
Lynch, Lauren Brie, 56

M

mac and cheese
    Dynamite Mac & Cheese Balls, 111
    Mac & Cheese Burger and Fries, 38–40
    Mac Wrap with Smoked Pastrami, 107
    Pepperoni Pizza Mac & Cheese, 73
    Shrimp Big Mac 'n' Cheese Burger, 41–43
    The Steez Dog, 56
macaroni
    Dynamite Mac & Cheese Balls, 111
    Mac-and-Cheese Buns, 40
    Mac & Cheese Burger and Fries, 38–40
    Mac Wrap with Smoked Pastrami, 107
    Pepperoni Pizza Mac & Cheese, 73
    Shrimp Big Mac 'n' Cheese Burger, 41–43
Macchina
    Burrata Pizza, 60
    Shrimp Scampi Pizza, 70
Mac Wrap with Smoked Pastrami, 107
mango
    Mango Habanero Bacon Wings, 84
    Mango Habanero Sauce, 84
maple syrup
    Maple-Butter Potato Chips, 142
    Milk 'N Chips, 142
    Pancake Burrito, 103
    Scrapple & Egg Burger, 52
    Wake and Bake Burger, 48
marinara sauce
    Marinara, 24
    The Panino Supremo Sandwich, 24
    Pepperoni Pizza Cheesesteak, 16
mascarpone cheese: Pancake Burrito, 103
Milk 'N Chips, 142
Mom's Kitchen & Bar, 103
Monterey jack cheese
    Cheese and Scallion Waffles, 134
    Loaded Carne Asada Quesadillas, 99
    Pepperoni Pizza Mac & Cheese, 73
    Shrimp Big Mac 'n' Cheese Burger, 41–43

The Steez Dog, 56
Morgan's Brooklyn Barbecue, 84
Morton, Annie, 47
mozzarella cheese
    Buffalo Chicken Pizza, 69
    Bulgogi Cheesesteak Tacos, 100
    Burrata Pizza, 60
    Cheese Sauce, 33
    Chopped Cheese Hero, 33
    Dominican Pizza, 63–64
    Extra Cheesy Garlic Knots, 115
    Kale Pesto–Stuffed Burrata, 116–118
    Kettle Queso, 96
    Mac-and-Cheese Buns, 40
    Mac & Cheese Burger and Fries, 38–40
    Nashville Hot Chicken Pizza, 65–66
    The Panino Supremo Sandwich, 24
    Pepperoni Pizza Cheesesteak, 16
    Pepperoni Pizza Mac & Cheese, 73
    Shrimp Scampi Pizza, 70
    Steak Burrito with Kettle Queso, 94–96
mushroom soup
    Cheese Sauce, 33
    Chopped Cheese Hero, 33

N

nacho cheese sauce
    Dynamite Mac & Cheese Balls, 111
    Texas Hotdog, 44
nachos: Chicken Tinga Nachos, 119–121
Nashville Hot Chicken Pizza, 65–66
New York Burger Co., 51
Nutella: Nutella Currant Jam, 138

O

oats: Wookies, 141
Oaxaca cheese
    Kettle Queso, 96
    Steak Burrito with Kettle Queso, 94–96
Olley, Matt, 112
onions
    Bacon Onion Jam, 55
    Bacon Onion Jam "Magic" Smash Burger, 55
    Beer Cheese, 47
    Beer Cheese Burger, 47
    Bronson Fries, 125
    Bulgogi Cheesesteak Tacos, 100
    Burger Sauce, 55
    The Butch Hero, 19
    Charred Pork Ribs, 91
    Cheese Sauce, 33
    Chicken Tinga Nachos, 119–121
    Chili, 44, 51
    Chili Cheeseburger, 51
    Chimichurri Sauce, 63
    Chopped Cheese Hero, 33
    Dominican Pizza, 63–64
    General Tso's Pig Wings, 88

Grilled BBQ Buffalo Wings with Alabama White Sauce, 81–83
Guacamole, 94, 97
Hoisin Barbecue Sauce, 91
Impossible™ Tacos, 104
Loaded Carne Asada Quesadillas, 97–99
Mango Habanero Sauce, 84
Pepperoni Pizza Cheesesteak, 16
Philly Cheesesteak, 23
Scrapple & Egg Burger, 52
Steak Burrito with Kettle Queso, 94–96
Taco Sauce, 104
Texas Hotdog, 44
Tomato Salsa, 97
Tomato Sauce, 63

P

Pancake Burrito, 103
pancetta
    Dominican Pizza, 63–64
    Tomato Sauce, 63
The Panino Supremo Sandwich, 24
panko crumbs
    Dynamite Mac & Cheese Balls, 111
    Fried Pickles, 129
    Mac-and-Cheese Buns, 40
    Mac & Cheese Burger and Fries, 38–40
parmesan cheese
    Extra Cheesy Garlic Knots, 115
    Kale Pesto, 116
    Kale Pesto–Stuffed Burrata, 116–118
    Mac-and-Cheese Buns, 40
    Mac & Cheese Burger and Fries, 38–40
    Pepperoni Pizza Cheesesteak, 16
pasta
    Lobster Burrata Pasta, 74
    The Steez Dog, 56
pastrami
    The Butch Hero, 19
    Mac Wrap with Smoked Pastrami, 107
PB&J Chicken 'N Waffles, 132–134
pecorino cheese: Burrata Pizza, 60
pepper jack cheese
    The Butch Hero, 19
    Loaded Doritos® Grilled Cheese, 20
    Pepperoni Pizza Mac & Cheese, 73
    Shrimp Big Mac 'n' Cheese Burger, 41–43
pepperoni
    Pepperoni Pizza Cheesesteak, 16
    Pepperoni Pizza Mac & Cheese, 73
Peterson, David, 47
Philly Cheesesteak, 23
The Pickle Guys, 129
pickles
    Bacon Onion Jam "Magic" Smash Burger, 55
    Fried Pickles, 129
    Nashville Hot Chicken Pizza, 65–66
pico de gallo
    Bulgogi Cheesesteak Tacos, 100

Loaded Doritos® Grilled Cheese, 20
Pig Beach
    Bacon Onion Jam "Magic" Smash Burger, 55
    Grilled BBQ Buffalo Wings with Alabama White Sauce, 81–83
pinto beans
    Chili, 44
    Texas Hotdog, 44
pizza
    Buffalo Chicken Pizza, 69
    Burrata Pizza, 60
    Detroit Pizza Dough, 65
    Dominican Pizza, 63–64
    Nashville Hot Chicken Pizza, 65–66
    Pepperoni Pizza Cheesesteak, 16
    Pepperoni Pizza Mac & Cheese, 73
    Shrimp Scampi Pizza, 70
plantains
    Dominican Pizza, 63–64
    Smashed Plantain Patacon with Roast Pork, 29–30
poblano peppers
    Chili, 51
    Chili Cheeseburger, 51
pork sausage: Pancake Burrito, 103
pork shanks: General Tso's Pig Wings, 88
pork shoulder: Smashed Plantain Patacon with Roast Pork, 29–30
pork spare ribs: Charred Pork Ribs, 91
potatoes
    Bronson Fries, 125
    Fries with the Works, 122
    Mac & Cheese Burger and Fries, 38–40
    Maple-Butter Potato Chips, 142
    Milk 'N Chips, 142
    Sake-Battered Fish & Chips Sando, 34
    Salt and Vinegar Chips, 34
provolone cheese
    Bulgogi Cheesesteak Tacos, 100
    Pepperoni Pizza Cheesesteak, 16
Pulled Chicken Sandwich, 27–28

Q

quesadillas: Loaded Carne Asada Quesadillas, 97–99
queso de freír
    Dominican Pizza, 63–64
    Smashed Plantain Patacon with Roast Pork, 29–30

R

radishes: Chicken Tinga Nachos, 119–121
Rallis, George, 34
ranch dressing: The Butch Hero, 19
Rawlinson, Sean, 38, 60, 70, 116, 119, 138
red bell peppers
    Bulgogi Cheesesteak Tacos, 100
    Cheese Sauce, 33

Chili, 44, 51
Chili Cheeseburger, 51
Chili Sauce, 78
Chimichurri Sauce, 63
Chopped Cheese Hero, 33
Dominican Pizza, 63–64
Firecracker Wings, 78–80
Pepperoni Pizza Cheesesteak, 16
Texas Hotdog, 44
red onions
    Chimichurri Sauce, 63
    Dominican Pizza, 63–64
    Guacamole, 97
    Loaded Carne Asada Quesadillas, 97–99
    Tomato Salsa, 97
ribs: Charred Pork Ribs, 91
rice
    Charred Pork Ribs, 91
    Steak Burrito with Kettle Queso, 94–96
Richman, Adam, 11, 33
Rodriguez, Stephen "Chef Papi," 33, 63
Roebling Sporting Club
    Chicken Tinga Nachos, 119–121
    French Toast Fritters, 138

S

Sake-Battered Fish & Chips Sando, 34
salami: Dominican Pizza, 63–64
salsa
    Salsa Fresca, 119
    Tomato Salsa, 97
sandwiches
    The Butch Hero, 19
    Chopped Cheese Hero, 33
    Loaded Doritos® Grilled Cheese, 20
    The Panino Supremo Sandwich, 24
    Pepperoni Pizza Cheesesteak, 16
    Philly Cheesesteak, 23
    Pulled Chicken Sandwich, 27–28
    Sake-Battered Fish & Chips Sando, 34
    Smashed Plantain Patacon with Roast Pork, 29–30
sauces
    Alabama White Sauce, 81
    Bacon Onion Jam, 55
    Blackened Chili Hot Sauce, 27
    Buffalo Wing Sauce, 83
    Burger Sauce, 55
    Cheese Sauce, 33, 119
    Chili Garlic Sauce, 27
    Chili Sauce, 78
    Chimichurri Sauce, 63
    General Tso Sauce, 88
    Grape Jelly "Jam," 132
    Hoisin Barbecue Sauce, 91
    Hot Honey, 112
    Kale Pesto, 116
    Mango Habanero Sauce, 84
    Papi's Sauce, 33, 63
    Paprika Aioli, 38

Peanut Sauce, 132
Salsa Verde Hot Sauce, 97
Shrimp Sauce, 41
Taco Sauce, 104
Tomato Sauce, 60, 63
Vinegar BBQ Sauce, 83
White Sauce, 66
Yuzu Tartar Sauce, 34
sausage
Dominican Pizza, 63–64
Pancake Burrito, 103
scallions
Bulgogi Cheesesteak Tacos, 100
Cheese and Scallion Waffles, 134
Firecracker Wings, 78–80
General Tso's Pig Wings, 88
PB&J Chicken 'N Waffles, 132–134
Shrimp Scampi Pizza, 70
The Steez Dog, 56
Texas Hotdog, 44
Schmackary's, 135
Schmahl, Zachary "Schmackary," 135
Scrapple & Egg Burger, 52
seasoning mixes
Blackening Seasoning, 38
Burger Seasoning, 51
Kentucky Fried Cauliflower Spice Blend, 112
Original Creole Seasoning, 38
Poultry Seasoning, 81
Spicy Seasoning Mix, 24, 122
SET L.E.S., 100
shallots
Pepperoni Pizza Mac & Cheese, 73
Shrimp Big Mac 'n' Cheese Burger, 41–43
Shrimp Scampi Pizza, 70
shrimp
Shrimp Big Mac 'n' Cheese Burger, 41–43
Shrimp Scampi Pizza, 70
Silver Light Tavern, 34, 112
Slow-Cooked Bourbon-Glazed Bacon, 126
Smashed Plantain Patacon with Roast Pork, 29–30
Smoky Manhattan Wings, 87
sourdough bread: Loaded Doritos® Grilled Cheese, 20
spaghetti: Lobster Burrata Pasta, 74
Steak Burrito with Kettle Queso, 94–96
The Steez Dog, 56
sweets
French Toast Fritters, 138
Funfetti Cookie Cakes, 135–137
Milk 'N Chips, 142
PB&J Chicken 'N Waffles, 132–134
Wookies, 141
Swiss cheese
Loaded Doritos® Grilled Cheese, 20
Mac-and-Cheese Buns, 40

Mac & Cheese Burger and Fries, 38–40
Pepperoni Pizza Cheesesteak, 16
The Steez Dog, 56

T

tacos
Bulgogi Cheesesteak Tacos, 100
Impossible™ Tacos, 104
Tang, Mikey, 100
Texas Hotdog, 44
Thual, David, 41, 73
tomatillos: Salsa Verde Hot Sauce, 97
tomatoes
Beer Cheese Burger, 47
Burrata Pizza, 60
Cheese Sauce, 33
Chicken Tinga Nachos, 119–121
Chili, 44, 51
Chili Cheeseburger, 51
Chopped Cheese Hero, 33
Dominican Pizza, 63–64
Firecracker Wings, 78–80
Impossible™ Tacos, 104
Loaded Carne Asada Quesadillas, 97–99
Marinara, 24
The Panino Supremo Sandwich, 24
Salsa Fresca, 119
Shrimp Big Mac 'n' Cheese Burger, 41–43
Smashed Plantain Patacon with Roast Pork, 29–30
Steak Burrito with Kettle Queso, 94–96
Taco Sauce, 104
Texas Hotdog, 44
Tomato Salsa, 97
Tomato Sauce, 60, 63
tomato paste
Chili, 44
Texas Hotdog, 44
tomato sauce
Burrata Pizza, 60
Chili, 44
Dominican Pizza, 63–64
Texas Hotdog, 44
The Truffleist, 16
turkey: The Butch Hero, 19

V

Velveeta Cheese Sauce: Mac Wrap with Smoked Pastrami, 107
Vidalia onions: Bacon Onion Jam, 55
Vigneulle, Chad, 20, 48
Villalobos, Jesus, 29, 44
Vinegar BBQ Sauce, 83
Vlasic, Franco, 87

W

Wake and Bake Burger, 48

walnuts
Kale Pesto, 116
Kale Pesto–Stuffed Burrata, 116–118
whiskey: Wookies, 141
white chocolate: Wookies, 141
white onions
Bacon Onion Jam "Magic" Smash Burger, 55
Beer Cheese, 47
Beer Cheese Burger, 47
Burger Sauce, 55
Cheese Sauce, 33
Chicken Tinga Nachos, 119–121
Chopped Cheese Hero, 33
Dominican Pizza, 63–64
Guacamole, 94
Impossible™ Tacos, 104
Mango Habanero Sauce, 84
Salsa Fresca, 119
Steak Burrito with Kettle Queso, 94–96
Taco Sauce, 104
Tomato Sauce, 63
Williamson, Rob, 103
wine
Lobster Burrata Pasta, 74
Sake-Battered Fish & Chips Sando, 34
Shrimp Scampi Pizza, 70
Smashed Plantain Patacon with Roast Pork, 29–30
Wing Jawn
General Tso's Pig Wings, 88
Scrapple & Egg Burger, 52
wings
Charred Pork Ribs, 91
Firecracker Wings, 78–80
General Tso's Pig Wings, 88
Grilled BBQ Buffalo Wings with Alabama White Sauce, 81–83
Mango Habanero Bacon Wings, 84
Smoky Manhattan Wings, 87
Wookies, 141

Y

yellow onions
Bronson Fries, 125
The Butch Hero, 19
Charred Pork Ribs, 91
Chili, 44
General Tso's Pig Wings, 88
Hoisin Barbecue Sauce, 91
Loaded Carne Asada Quesadillas, 97–99
Pepperoni Pizza Cheesesteak, 16
Philly Cheesesteak, 23
Salsa Verde Hot Sauce, 97
Texas Hotdog, 44

Z

Zisimatos, Christos, 51